THE ALIEN ANIMALS

The Natural History Press, publisher for The American Museum of Natural History, is a division of Doubleday and Company, Inc. Directed by a joint editorial board made up of members of the staff of both the Museum and Doubleday, the Natural History Press publishes books and periodicals in all branches of the life and earth sciences, including anthropology and astronomy. The Natural History Press has its editorial offices at The American Museum of Natural History, Central Park West at 79th Street, New York 24, New York, and its business offices at 501 Franklin Avenue, Garden City, New York.

THE ALIEN ANIMALS

GEORGE LAYCOCK

PUBLISHED FOR
THE AMERICAN MUSEUM OF NATURAL HISTORY
THE NATURAL HISTORY PRESS
GARDEN CITY, NEW YORK

ACKNOWLEDGMENTS

To all those individuals and organizations who so kindly helped me during the preparation of this book I want to express my sincere and grateful appreciation. I especially want to thank those who helped by reading portions of the manuscript, made research materials available and gave their time for interviews. The following list includes some of those to whom I am deeply indebted for valuable assistance.

Dr. Clarence Cottam of the Welder Wildlife Foundation, Professor H. S. Swingle of Auburn University, Dr. Herbert W. Levi of the Museum of Comparative Zoology Harvard University, Dr. Frederick Hamerstrom of the Wisconsin Conservation Department, Dr. Tony J. Peterle of the Ohio State University Department of Zoology, R. Roy Keaton of the American Medical Association, Robert A. Jantzen of the Arizona Game and Fish Department, Dr. C. Richard Robins of the Institute of Marine Science, Dr. Kazimierz Wodzicki of the Animal Ecology Division of the New Zealand Department of Scientific and Industrial Research, The New Mexico Department of Game and Fish, The Wisconsin Conservation Department, The Michigan Department of Conservation, The Indiana Department of Conservation, and the Missouri Conservation Commission.

Contents

LIST OF ILLUSTRATIONS

THE ALIEN ANIMALS

"I have given you lands to hunt in,
I have given you streams to fish in,
I have given you bear and bison,
I have given you roe and reindeer,
I have given you brant and beaver,
Filled the marshes full of wild-fowl,
Filled the rivers full of fishes;
Why then are you not contented?"

The Song of Hiawatha
HENRY WADSWORTH LONGFELLOW

Chapter 1

The Animal Movers

———— ❧ ————

MAN has long considered himself capable of improving upon nature. He often regards nature's distribution of her creatures as haphazard or at best unfortunate. He looks about himself and, with absolute confidence in his own judgment, says, "That animal seems made to order for the Midwest." He has moved birds halfway around the earth to eat some insect they did not like, introduced rabbits to foreign countries where they created barren lands, imported and released huge furbearers in pursuit of wealth.

It may have begun with Noah, but, wherever it started, the whole idea of rearranging the earth's wild creatures still seems irresistible. Man, the supreme meddler, has never been quite satisfied with the world as he found it, and as he has dabbled in rearranging it to his own design, he has frequently created surprising and frightening situations for himself.

In many instances, wildlife introductions have been unintentional. Rats and mice have gone around the world in ships' holds. Insects are notorious for their unwelcome invasions of new lands, and we maintain costly quarantines to guard against such pests. In 1776 two brigades of Hessian soldiers arrived in North America to assist General William Howe in subduing the unruly colonists. Although the Revolutionary forces managed to cope with the Hessians, a small gnat that came along in their straw mattresses is still a major enemy of American wheat farmers. The Hessian fly destroys about

$16,000,000 worth of wheat annually in the United States. The Pilgrims escorted the clothes moth into the country in their woolen garments, and the annual losses to these, and other imported fabric pests, have been computed at more than $200,000,000 a year.

Meanwhile, man's drastic altering of the landscape has enabled still other animals to occupy and flourish in new territories where they were previously excluded by natural barriers. One dramatic recent example is the sea lamprey. Not until the Welland Ship Canal created a Niagara Falls by-pass in 1921 were sea lampreys able to invade the Great Lakes to the west. The lamprey population explosion that followed decimated the valuable lake trout. The invaders were controlled only after many years of work and the expenditure of huge sums of money.

Aside from domestic animals and those that have slipped in as unwanted aliens, there are the wild creatures men have transplanted purposely from one part of the world to another.

What has motivated men to import and release foreign species of wildlife? Some species are moved for reasons of sentiment. In the 1950s a citizen of Kent, Ohio, decided the handsome black squirrels normally found in more northern latitudes would be interesting in his hometown in Ohio. The breeding stock he brought in and released prospered and within a few years people who had originally encouraged the squirrels were searching for methods of destroying them. Such intentional introductions of new and foreign elements into wildlife communities are the manipulations of nature with which this book is concerned. In an almost casual manner, men have moved the world's wild deer, swine, foxes, antelopes, rabbits, squirrels, snails, snakes, moose, buffalo, musk ox, and all manner of other creatures, each the custodian of its own diseases and parasites, to new lands where they felt these animals should have been placed but were not. The animal movers go about their business as enthusiastically today as ever. With a world of past mistakes to guide them, they ignore the warnings of history—like gamblers always searching and hoping to hit that exotic wildlife jackpot. There has been enough success with a few creatures, including the ringneck pheasant and the brown trout, to keep hope alive.

It is much easier, however, to find examples the animal movers would prefer to ignore. The history of wildlife management and manipulation is replete with case histories that emphasize the harm such projects can cause. Release of wildlife into territory foreign to it involves, not a calculated risk, but a risk too great to calculate. The animal moving game, however, proceeds through the land.

Chapter 2

Strangers in the Southwest

On December 15, 1950, when the New Mexico State Game Commission assembled in Santa Fe for its regular monthly meeting, the business was routine—except for one uncommon item. It was during this meeting that department director Elliot S. Barker told the commission about Joe McKnight and the Barbary sheep.

McKnight, who ranched over on the Hondo River near Picacho, enjoyed having his Herefords and horses co-mingle in the pastures with a variety of foreign game animals. Among his favorite foreign imports was the rugged Barbary sheep, about which Barker spoke in glowing terms to the commission. Barker had already agreed with McKnight that this shaggy creature which sometimes weighs more than 300 pounds should be turned free in New Mexico's high arid desert country in hopes it would prosper and provide the state's hunters with African-style trophies right in their home state.

In fact, Barker had not come before the commission to ask if he might release these exotic sheep. The deed was already done. Several months earlier, personnel from the Department of Game and Fish had trapped four ewes and four rams from McKnight's big enclosure. These had been hauled over to the Canadian River Canyon and given their freedom. Barker obtained the commission's stamp of approval on what he had done, and to this day the State Game Commission has not wavered in its enthusiam for the idea. It has, in fact, broadened its horizons and extended the search for other large foreign mammals that might find a niche in the wilds of New Mexico. That state's enthusiasm, however, has not always been echoed, nor its animal imports appreciated in adjoining states.

In its native North Africa the Barbary sheep, which is also known as the aoudad, inhabits the parched southern slopes of the Great Atlas Mountains. Stretched out below it are the sands of the Sahara. Hot winds rise up from the desert to altitudes of 6500 feet and more, where the sheep live. In this harsh climate the Barbary sheep, say the Arabs, are content to drink once every four or five days.

Barbary sheep were first imported to this country about 1900, for zoos in New York and Washington. Zoo managers soon learned that these African sheep breed readily in captivity. They reproduced so rapidly that the flocks had to be reduced by a third to a half every year. The meat went to feed the lions and tigers.

Soon every zoo that wanted Barbary sheep had them. When New Mexico decided to go into the African wild-game business, it conducted a survey of all states to see where these animals might then have been living. "Herds of from six to 200," said the New Mexico report, "were reported to be in zoological gardens or private game farms in California, Connecticut, Maryland, Michigan, New Mexico, North Dakota, Wisconsin and Toronto, Canada."

Joe McKnight, up on the Hondo, had started his herd in 1940, with Barbary sheep purchased from zoos in St. Louis, Missouri, and San Diego, California. He installed them in a 200-acre pasture and they reproduced so rapidly that a few years later he moved them to a 2000-acre enclosure.

If Barbary sheep were, as reports stated, conditioned to living in rugged terrain, the Canadian River Canyon area seemed cut to their specifications. The Canadian River Canyon is sixty miles long, from 300 to 800 feet deep, and its slopes vary between fifty and seventy-five per cent. At the top of the canyon on either side a sheer face of granite forms a wall thirty to seventy-five feet high. Deep rocky gorges and ledges extend back from either wall of the canyon, and on these the native mule deer, as well as the African newcomers, find vegetation to support them. Here and there steep and difficult trails lead down into the canyon.

To the New Mexico wildlife specialists eight sheep did not seem sufficient. They began a search for more Barbary sheep to reinforce the original planting. Barker arranged to buy twenty-seven ewes and seventeen rams from the William Randolph Hearst ranch in California. "They cost twenty-five dollars a head," he reported to the State Game Commission, "plus trucking." These were released a short distance upstream from the first planting. "We did not want to put them in a place," said Barker, "where they would mix with our native bighorn sheep."

The Barbary sheep is a big animal. Males have been known to reach a weight of 320 pounds. Both sexes have horns. The horns of the male Barbary sheep grow to two and a half feet or more in length, with a spread of thirty inches—greater than that of any of our native North American wild sheep.

The Barbary sheep stands somewhat higher at the shoulders than he does in the rear. The coat of both sexes is a sandy brown color. There is no large patch of white on this animal and consequently he blends into the rocky or desert background.

The Barbary sheep wears a mane on the front of his neck. In the older animals the long hair of his mane sometimes hangs almost to the ground. In addition, these animals have a similar fringe along the front of each foreleg, like a cowboy's chaps.

Once the fifty-two transplanted Barbary sheep had been released in the Canadian River Canyon, wildlife specialists waited expectantly to see what would happen. "It is impossible," said New Mexico wildlife biologist Herman A. Ogren, "to predict how the Barbary sheep populations will react in New Mexico. To learn this it would seem necessary that we allow the Barbary sheep population to take its course."

Finally, four years after the release, the Department of Game and Fish sent a three-man crew into the canyon on horseback and foot to find out what the Barbary sheep were doing. In three days of scrambling over rocky slopes, the sheep counters located forty Barbary sheep. Barbary sheep, they soon discovered, have a habit of hiding from observers. Like the native bighorn sheep, they frequently utilize overhanging rocks or caves to keep out of sight. The first sheep the three-man crew located, a band of fourteen, were hiding in a cave thirty feet long, twenty feet deep, and six feet high. The sheep had bedded down.

It would seem obvious that the animals would be difficult to count from an airplane, but there was no way to be certain without trying it. District Biologist Jim McClellan decided to fly the canyon if he could find a pilot willing to risk the flight. The local pilot who agreed to the plan suggested they begin at the upper end where the canyon walls are so close together that there is not room for the plane's wings to fit between them. "As the canyon became wider than the wing span of the plane," McClellan reported, "the plane was flown lower into the canyon until it was below the rim." The little two-seater skimmed through the canyon within fifty feet of the creek bed while the pilot flew with half-flaps to slow the speed of the plane and give McClellan all possible opportunity to see sheep. Soon he had spotted a band of twenty-five mature rams. They dashed beneath an overhanging ledge and hid from sight. So closely do these creatures stick to their hiding places that one, secluded beneath the limbs of a juniper, refused to move even when the pilot brushed the wheels of his plane through the top of the tree. Before the aerial census was completed, however, McClellan had counted sixty-five Barbary sheep.

Next came an eight-day search from the ground. As a result of these three counts, New Mexico wildlife biologists decided there were now perhaps 200 Barbary sheep living in the Canadian River Gorge, a figure that seems reasonable.

The New Mexico wildlife managers also knew that in four years Barbary sheep had spread out to occupy forty-five miles of the canyon. They have never been greatly concerned, however, about the possibility that the African sheep would spread beyond the canyon where they were planted. From each rim of the canyon a shortgrass prairie spotted here and there with piñon juniper and scrub oak stretches out for miles and offers scant opportunity for an animal the size of a Barbary sheep to hide. Ranchers reported occasions when the sheep were seen feeding at dawn on the edge of these prairies. But at the first sight of man they slipped back over the lip of the canyon where they could hide among the granite boulders.

Aeons of evolutionary development fitted the Barbary sheep well for traveling under these difficult conditions. Once excited they break into a fast run and gracefully bound over large boulders or leap a dozen feet or more from one narrow ledge to the next. They travel in single file where the going is rough. Where there is more room they run in tight bands, with their lambs in the center of the flock. Once they take refuge beneath some overhanging rock, the lambs hide beneath the bellies of the adult animals. By the time it is a day old, the lamb can dash along the ledges and over boulder-strewn slopes with its mother.

It became apparent to the New Mexico State Game Commission that the quickest way to gain information about the new sheep would be to open a hunting season for them. In the fall of 1957, Barbary sheep in the Canadian River Canyon were hunted for the first time. Between then and early 1960, four hunts were conducted, one in each of the four seasons with hunters selected by a lottery. The average number of hunters each time was sixty-one. The number of Barbary sheep shot, however, dropped steadily from forty-three taken during the first hunt to sixteen in the fourth hunt, so the commission ended the hunting of its cherished imports until it could once again be determined that their numbers could stand the pressure.

Meanwhile, they had learned a lot about this animal. Each hunter filled out a questionnaire before leaving the area, and each successful hunter collected and turned in one quart of the stomach contents from the animal he had taken. Now biologists, working in their laboratories, were able to identify foods the Barbary sheep were eating. They learned that the sheep wintered largely on such grasses as blue grama and little bluestem. In spring and summer they turned to browsing on mountain mahogany, oak, yucca, Apache-plume, mesquite, sage, and the fruit of prickly pear.

What might ultimately become of this animal in New Mexico, or in surrounding states into which it might spread? New Mexico officials expect that hunting for Barbary sheep will be restricted to the northeastern part of the state for several years. They see slight possibility that the sheep will spread beyond areas where it is desired, and they are convinced that it could be quickly brought under control by hunting if it threatened to get out of bounds.

In spite of their obvious satisfaction over the establishment of Barbary sheep, New Mexico wildlife biologists are alert for any damage it might inflict on the remnant populations of native bighorns which still persist in the wilder parts of the state. So close have these American bighorn sheep come to extinction that estimates currently place their numbers in New Mexico at fewer than 200 head.

According to Levon Lee, Assistant Chief of Game Management of the New Mexico Department of Game and Fish, "Our main concern from the game management aspect is to keep a wary eye upon this animal since we are receiving consistent reports of their widespread distribution in the state."

"If this animal were to scatter all over the state and intermingle with our other big game on their ranges, it could cause some serious problems. . . ."

One of the biggest fears expressed by Lee was that the Barbary sheep might bring parasites and diseases to share with the native wildlife. "The Barbary sheep," he told a meeting of the Desert Bighorn Council at Las Cruces, New Mexico, in April 1960, "is very heavily parasitized with both ectoparasites and endoparasites. Living as they have in the heavily populated North African coast and being in contact with horses, mules, camels, dogs, pigs, sheep, goats and wild game, they have evidently been able to survive infestation with parasites common to one or more of all these animals. A list of their endoparasites sounds like a small monograph on the helminths.

"The possibility of the Barbary sheep transmitting some of these very undesirable parasites to other game or to domestic livestock is, if it were to be the case, rather frightening. It would be particularly so in the case of the native bighorn sheep, which are happily free of the more pathogenic parasites. . . . We are determined at all cost," Lee added, "to keep the Barbary sheep off the range of the desert bighorn or the Rocky Mountain bighorn. Aggressive, competitive, shy, and wild, they could well displace the two native species of bighorn sheep."

"Our men in the field," he concluded, "have a standing order that if they find a Barbary anywhere in known bighorn sheep range to lay him down."

This concern does not end at the state borders. What would happen to the Barbary sheep that crossed a state line? "If he went into Texas," says Lee, "he would probably get along all right." Texas already has a small band of these sheep in its rugged Palo Duro Canyon not far from Amarillo. "But if he wandered into Arizona, I think he would be in trouble."

This could be an understatement. The Arizona wildlife people have left no doubts as to their antagonism toward the free-running African game. Arizona's Chief of Game Management, Robert A. Jantzen, says, "We have had unsubstantiated reports that Barbary sheep have crossed the line into Arizona. We will attempt to eliminate them if they are observed in Arizona." He pointed out that Arizona laws leave the Barbary sheep completely unprotected there and added that ". . . we have no plans to change that status. If New Mexico sheep ranges are like ours," Jantzen added, "I think Barbary sheep would have a definite competitive and detrimental influence on bighorn on common range."

In June 1963 the Western Association of State Game and Fish Commissioners expressed some of Jantzen's thinking in a resolution warning against stocking exotic game mammals before thorough studies could be made of their effect on existing populations of both wildlife and vegetation.

Meanwhile the Desert Bighorn Council, an organization including bighorn sheep specialists from many western states and Mexico, adopted a resolution calling for tighter controls on releases of exotic ungulates.

But in spite of such misgivings about the hazards inherent in the Barbary sheep program, Levon Lee is probably right when he says, "The Barbary sheep is undoubtedly here to stay. We're happy," says Lee, "and satisfied that this adds an important game animal to what we have in New Mexico."

So happy was New Mexico with its big shaggy African sheep, in fact, that its officials began looking over the long list of other African big game animals. One of the stanchest advocates of bringing African species over to keep the Barbary sheep company under New Mexico's bright blue skies was Dr. Frank C. Hibben, a professor from Albuquerque and a member of the New Mexico Game and Fish Commission. At his urging the commission considered several animals that seemed suitable for New Mexico. They selected the Siberian ibex, relative of the domestic goat, the elk-sized greater kudu, and the cantankerous unpredictable oryx.

In a commission meeting late in 1962, Dr. Hibben, who

had hunted in Africa, described the kudu and its plight. Here was an animal that had formerly ranged over most of southern Africa but which was rapidly being exterminated. Citizens of recently formed African nations, suddenly freed from restrictions on killing wild animals, were slaughtering the kudu and other creatures in frightening numbers. Dr. Hibben suggested that the commission buy eight kudu. The price was $1500 each F.O.B. Clifton, New Jersey. The rest of the commission members quickly agreed. If they changed their minds there was little doubt that they could readily sell the animals to zoos and recover their investment.

The kudu, which is grayish in color and wears a pair of great spiral-shaped horns, possesses fabulous stamina and strength. He can clear an eight-foot fence from a standing position. The method used to capture them on the African plains is both simple and risky. Because they run like a quarter horse on the short dash, Landrovers are used to run them down. When the vehicle is alongside a kudu, an animal catcher riding the outside of the car drops a noose over the kudu's neck. The noose is attached to the end of a long pole. Now the car jerks to a halt. The captive is thrown and held down by a crowd of helpers until it can be forced into a crate. But it is still a long way to New Mexico.

First there is an official two-month quarantine in the land of origin. This is followed by an ocean voyage and then another thirty-day quarantine at the U. S. Department of Agriculture quarantine station in Clifton, New Jersey. But government regulations say these animals must, as a protection against carrying foreign diseases to livestock, spend the rest of their lives in approved zoological gardens. There is, however, no regulation against releasing their offspring into the wild. The New Mexico State Game Commission made an agreement with the Albuquerque Zoo: the zoo would keep the imported animals and the commission would have the offspring.

Fifteen kudus were captured, crated, and loaded on trucks

headed for the quarantine station. In this barren land where rain in any quantity is a rarity, a sudden cloudburst washed out the road and caused the truckload of crated animals to turn over. Three of the kudus died in the wreck. The animal exporter and his crews turned back to Africa in a vain effort to replace the lost animals.

Eventually the animals, having cleared their quarantine period, were loaded aboard a ship and lashed to the deck in their crates. When they had almost completed the journey, the ship turned back to avoid a hurricane. The storm chased the ship all the way back to the Azores—with the kudus still lashed to the deck. It is testimony to their stamina that they eventually landed, cleared quarantine in New Jersey, and survived a five-day truck trip in their original crates to the zoo in Albuquerque.

In due time the Albuquerque Zoo had acquired ten new kudus purchased with money from hunting and fishing license sales. Before long there were also nine Siberian ibexes in the zoo. Next the department set about the difficult task of securing the oryx from their native territory in the incredibly dry and barren Kalahari Desert.

With its seed stock now safely ensconced in the zoo and its hopes high, New Mexico's State Game Commission next ordered the construction of a 320-acre holding pen in the rugged isolated country where the Gila River breaks out of its box canyon 440 miles south of Santa Fe. Here is where the offspring of the immigrant kudu and the oryx will come for conditioning before they are turned loose in the wilds of New Mexico.

As New Mexico wildlife biologists see it, this area provides an ideal release site for their transported African big game. The plains around the area are at 5000 feet above sea level and the granitic mountain reserved for the oryx and the kudu rises to 10,000 feet. Here the oryx would find the open, gravelly rolling desert country similar to that occupied by his kind in Africa, and the kudu, at home in the thickets, could live along the watercourses where the thick-growing brush provides the thorny types of vegetation he favors.

As for the predators these animals might encounter, the kudu seemed big enough to take care of his own. His neighbor, the oryx, should survive on pure cussedness. "The coyotes," said Levon Lee, "are in for a surprise if they tackle the oryx." By nature, the oryx is capable and willing to fight all comers from the moment he is able to stand on his own legs. A newborn oryx has been known to attack the attending veterinarian in the zoo. Their horn buds are already evident when they are born. If attacked by a predator, the oryx gives a lion-like roar and attacks the carnivore with his sharp hoofs and horns. As Levon Lee said, "We figure they will suffer very little predation."

Farther south, on either side of the Rio Grande, private citizens are busily importing foreign animals in a variety that makes the New Mexico State Game Commission program look conservative. Near Nuevo Laredo, Mexico, just across the Rio Grande from Texas, is the 7000-acre holding of the Longorias, a family of imaginative and successful ranchers and business people. One of the brothers, Octaviano Longoria, hunted in Africa, Alaska, and India and learned of the recent threat of extinction faced by various species of wildlife. He decided that the Longorias' rangeland could provide the salvation for some of these threatened creatures if they were brought to new homes in the historic valley of the Rio Grande.

As a result of this decision, a fantastic parade of foreign creatures have been tenderly installed on the holdings of the Longorias. As one might expect, along with the cape buffalo, Australian wallabies, Barbary sheep, Siberian yaks, zebras, and sika deer, there came camels, giraffes, and ostriches. All were turned out to roam the 7000-acre holdings.

Meanwhile, hundreds of foreign birds have been brought here and released free to fly wherever they like. Among the birds are partridges, flamingos, African secretary birds, and various doves and cranes. The ostriches, with characteristic ingratitude, seem to cause more than their share of trouble. One kicked a young camel to death. While such conflicts distress the Longorias, they do not discourage them. Most of their animals are either purchased from zoos or shipped in by dealers.

Local native predators, as one might have predicted, made early inroads on the new animals turned out inside the big ranch enclosure. Direct counterattacks were the answer. Bobcats and coyotes were killed at every opportunity. On one big neighborhood hunt it is said that 2800 coyotes were killed.

Meanwhile, the Longorias and the managers of the King Ranch at Kingville, Texas, worked out an agreement whereby they cooperate in their joint search for foreign animals to import to this continent. The King ranch has some wild animals of its own established on its sprawling holdings. Sharing those ranch lands with the famed Santa Gertrudis cattle are blackbuck, mouflon sheep, axis deer, eland, and the nilgai. And other ranchers on both sides of the river are engaged in similar projects, all of which adds up to what is happily described in some circles as "a little Africa along the Rio Grande."

Wildlife biologists surveying the exotic big-game populations in North America have said that Texas has become the home of more exotic ungulates than any comparable area of North America. One survey of exotic big-game animals in the state in 1964 revealed that forty-eight of the 254 counties in Texas now have established populations of foreign mammals. They are spreading over that state at a growing rate, and several species, including the nilgai, blackbuck, mouflon sheep, and Barbary sheep, are prospering in unfenced populations. In Texas the red deer numbers appear static. But this is not true of the nilgai, a large antelope originally from India. A dozen of these creatures are believed to have been turned out on a coastal ranch in South Texas in 1930. Today there are more than 3000 of them wandering over several adjoining ranches and a total of 1,425,000 acres. One census by wildlife biologists in Texas in 1964 listed a total of thirteen species of exotic ungulates.

Among the justifications frequently advanced for transplanting these African animals to American shores is the fact that some of them face early extinction in their native lands. In some distant future year men may draw on North American populations to restock these animals in their original range. What will happen to the native American wildlife sharing living space with them meanwhile is a question no man is capable of answering.

Some wildlife biologists, viewing developments in Texas and New Mexico, live with their fingers crossed. At stake are the native rangelands, the wildlife, the livestock industry, and perhaps human health. There is the ever-present threat that one or more of these foreign animals, suddenly relieved of its natural controls, might expand into plague proportions.

THE ELUSIVE PRIZE

Chapter 3

Saga of the Ringneck

————— 🌲 —————

JUDGE Owen Nickerson Denny had visited the busy harbor in Shanghai several times in recent days. Each time he went straight to the bark *Isle of Bute*. Down in the ship's dimly lighted hold he inspected again the unusual bamboo cage he had ordered installed there.

Workmen had constructed amidships a great enclosure twenty feet square. They had then spread a scow-load of fine gravel on the floor. Next they had carried in tubs in which growing bushes were planted, and they placed the shrubbery around the interior of the big bamboo cage. Nearby were supplies of small grains and also sacks of charcoal.

Then, shortly before the *Isle of Bute* slipped from the Shanghai harbor, workmen carried aboard several squat, round wicker baskets. Inside the bamboo enclosure they opened the wicker baskets and released ten beautifully colored, wild-caught, cock ringnecked pheasants and eighteen hens. This historic shipment of pioneering pheasants arrived safely in the harbor at Portland, Oregon, on March 13, 1882.

Back in Shanghai the news of the pheasants' safe arrival was Judge Denny's first taste of satisfaction in moving the pheasant. The judge hoped this little shipment of birds would establish wild breeding populations of pheasants in his home state. Other pheasant fanciers before him had tried transplanting them to the New World on many occasions, and each time the efforts resulted in failure. But this time, if Denny had it figured out right, might be different.

Unlike the jungle fowl, ancestor of the barnyard hen, the Chinese ringneck pheasant never fully yielded his wild free spirit to those who sought to domesticate him. It is one thing to keep a pheasant in a pen and quite another to tame him. This very wildness has endeared the bird to generations of gunners.

Biologists who caution the animal importers to go slowly, and warn of the serious biological and economic hazards which exotics can bring, are soon confronted with an argument designed to end all disagreement. They are promptly admonished to "look at the pheasant."

Whether or not the pheasant has been an unqualified success in this country is still debated in some circles. The saga of the ringneck is filled with adventure, tinged with romance and bordered with disappointments. The suggestion, however, has merit and consequently we shall, in this chapter, do as we have been advised and "look at the pheasant."

The pheasant is a hardy roughneck in the world of birds, adaptable to a wide variety of climates. The bird can live in varying degrees of prosperity from sea level to elevations of 8000 feet. Some withstand the scorching desert heat of the lower Imperial Valley of California and on into Baja California. But they do best in the level, fertile, high-producing agricultural lands, the grain fields of the Midwest and North Central states, and the irrigated valleys of western states.

Wherever the pheasant lives, he follows much the same pattern of activity. The male carries the family colors. His brilliant uniform and long tail mark him as one of the world's most colorful birds. The actual purpose for such a beautiful tail may be obscure to the human mind, assuming that it needs a purpose. But it is apparently important in the world of pheasants. Biologists have noticed that cock pheasants that have lost their tail feathers have a difficult time attracting a harem and may have to go through the summer unmated.

The males may begin to fight with each other and establish territories while the chill winds of February still whip
across the flatlands. By late May and early June, nesting has
reached its peak. The hens have chosen a place in meadow
or weed patch and lined a hollow depression with whatever
grass or weeds they could easily find. Here they deposit
their eggs, frequently a dozen or more. The setting hen
crouches there among the brown weeds and her somber
brown feathers help hide her. The chore of incubating the
eggs lasts twenty-three days.

Meanwhile, her well-dressed mate, who probably has three
or four other hens in his harem, abandons them all. The
long summer days, filled with responsibility and work for
the hen, find the male bird free to wander and feed at his
leisure, dust himself by the edge of the farm lane, and occasionally crow enough to remind the creatures of the countryside that the male pheasant is still in business. Mowing
machines and human beings may disrupt the nesting of the
female. Crows, snakes, skunks, and free-roaming cats and
dogs add their depredations.

Within an hour after hatching, the pheasant chicks are out
of the nest and running. At this moment they weigh less
than an ounce, but shortly they are searching out and consuming insects. When two months old they begin acquiring a
new set of feathers. The post-juvenile feathers of the young
male will, by autumn, replace his brown coat and decorate
him with the flashy colors of his father—and all in time for
the hunting season.

Pheasants began their travels long before they reached the
New World. The Romans carried them from the Orient at
a time now lost to history. Stock from the Roman Empire
was, in turn, transported to the British Isles, probably at the
command of Julius Caesar.

Here was the beginning of the sport of pheasant hunting in
the British Isles. Men learned the excitement of sending

arrows from their longbows, and bolts from their cross-bows, after the cackling pheasant on the rise.

Englishmen who immigrated to this country could not quickly forget the pheasant hunting they had known. The exuberant dash of the springer spaniels into the coverts followed by the nerve-tingling whir of the flushing birds were heady memories. The result of this longing was predictable.

There had been attempts to stock pheasants in the New World before George Washington was born. They had been released at least as early as 1730. During the time he was governor of New York, John Montgomerie turned out half a dozen pairs of pheasants on what is now Governors Island. The governor could give his birds or eggs away, as could those who received stock from him, but the poacher caught making inroads on these treasured pheasants could be fined ten shillings or five days in jail.

Later, Benjamin Franklin's son-in-law, Richard Bache, decided pheasants would add color to his estate in New Jersey. The pheasants he brought in and released, however, languished and disappeared.

Releases occurred in numerous estates throughout New England. Their fate was invariably the same. The birds eventually disappeared and with them went a margin of the hope that motivated their importers. In New Hampshire, Governor Wentworth is said to have turned loose several pairs of pheasants in 1793 to fly in the woodlands of his estate. But, as the record so succinctly explains, ". . . they have not since been seen."

These early efforts established the pattern. For the next century and a half men would continue their attempts to get these imported birds established in every part of the country—frequently with success, more often with failure. The birds that were to build the first successful pheasant population in North America came not from Europe but directly from the Orient, ancient ancestral homeland of the species. And they came, not to New England, but to the fertile irrigated farmlands of Oregon's Willamette Valley.

Owen Denny, who was responsible for this first successful American introduction of the now cherished game bird, was neither biologist nor explorer. He had no professional background in scientific study and lacked any extensive knowledge of the birds of the world.

Denny was by profession a lawyer. He had drifted into politics. Eventually his political reward included an assignment to the post of consul for the United States in Shanghai in 1877.

Judge Owen N. Denny, the new U.S. consul, adapted readily to his life in the Orient, as did his wife, Gertrude. A whole new and exciting world opened for them. While Mrs. Denny attended tea parties and wandered among the little shops purchasing hand-carved trinkets, the judge applied himself with vigor to the duties of his office. And it was not long before he rose to the post of consul general.

Now the Dennys lived in a fine house in Shanghai. They had servants who served them the finest of Oriental cooking. Among the dishes the Dennys most enjoyed was one known to relatively few Americans of that day—roast pheasant.

As might be predicted, Judge Denny began to feel that he could serve his country nobly by transplanting pheasants from the Orient to Oregon. On January 28, 1881, he sent the following message to his friend A. H. Morgan in Oregon. It is printed here with the permission of the Oregon Historical Society from an article by Virginia C. Holmgren in the September 1964 edition of the *Oregon Historical Quarterly*.

I mentioned in my last letter that it was my intention to try and stock our State with some of the finest varieties of game pheasants found in China, and to this end I have been collecting them for some months past.

I am sending by the ship Otago out of Port Townsend, Captain Royal commanding, about 60 Mongolian [Judge Denny is believed to have been in error in not properly calling these birds

"Chinese" pheasants.] pheasants to be turned loose in various sections of the state. . . .

These birds are delicious eating and very game and will furnish fine sport. I also send 11 Mongolian sand grouse. These birds have very peculiarly shaped feet—resembling some-what those of a mole. Next I send 7—all I could possibly obtain before the ship sailed—Chefoo partridges. I am collecting other varieties which I shall send in due time—some of them beautiful birds.

Will you please cooperate with the sportsmen clubs and see that due notice is given so that the "shootists" will not kill them?

Please lose no time in setting these birds at liberty as soon as they arrive . . .

Next I am sending 16 trees of the Pang Tao or flat peach. These trees bear very delicious fruit and will do well in Eastern Oregon. The fruit resembles a tomato. I also send a lot of bamboos. They will need to be planted in a rich, moist, sandy soil where they will get plenty of sun. I do not see why the bamboo should not do well in Oregon.

This shipment of pheasants, however, encountered rough times during the trip and arrived in poor condition. Before long, pheasants, Chefoo partridges, and sand grouse alike had disappeared. The bamboo, it is said, still prospers locally in Oregon. The news of the birds' failure was a sharp disappointment to the consul general. The experiment had cost him considerable time, plus $300 out of his own pocket. But he was a determined man, and fonder now than ever of the taste of roast pheasant.

With that initial effort, the judge had learned some things about pheasants. His second shipment would never have to cross the Pacific Ocean cramped in wicker baskets. He would build them a bamboo chicken pen that would permit them to travel first class.

This time Judge Denny had arranged for his brother John to receive the pheasants. John was to release them behind the old Denny home on Peterson Butte. As the judge's wife, Gertrude, wrote to her sister-in-law, "He thinks that perhaps the folks there will protect them for the sake of the Denny family, till they get a good start in the country."

By 1884, when Judge and Mrs. Denny returned to Portland, the pheasants were already spreading out into surrounding lands and crossing into adjoining counties. Within a few years people who had never before seen pheasants were watching the chicken-size birds strut along the irrigation ditches and slip through the weed patches. They spoke of them as the "Denny pheasants." It seemed they were showing up in startling numbers following each new nesting season.

The birds became so numerous that, a single decade after Judge Denny's second shipment of birds was turned loose, the state of Oregon established this country's first open season on pheasants. The year was 1891. Estimates of the number of pheasants taken during that first season place the total at 50,000. The pheasant had secured his place in the ranks of America's game birds.

Word of Oregon's pheasant bonanza spread rapidly. Even before the hunting season was first opened in the Willamette Valley, surplus birds were being live-trapped there for transplanting to other areas. They were turned out in western Washington, then eastern Washington, Idaho, and southern British Columbia. In 1911, Oregon began incubating pheasants at Corvallis, in one of the first large-scale, state-operated game farms in this country. Soon other states were to follow this example.

Within a relatively brief period hundreds of pheasants were turned out into the American countryside. They were released in every state. They were planted in mountains, deserts, farmlands, and woodlands. It was as if we possessed an endless supply of some golden seed. We sowed it in haphazard manner and stood back to await the happy results.

This was the only approach that occurred to most who worked with the pheasants. Surprisingly enough, many of their efforts accomplished precisely what they had desired. But what a waste this method proved! Of the forty-eight states in which pheasants were planted, they were successful in only eighteen. "Literally millions of hours of time, effort and money have been wasted in trying to put these birds where they did not belong," Dr. Gardiner Bump of the Fish and Wildlife Service has said, "millions that might better have been spent in improving conditions for our native game species."

State after state attempted to emulate Oregon's pheasant story. In California, as in most states, the earliest pheasant introductions were made by private individuals. The state government came into the picture in 1889 with its first release of 140 pheasants purchased at ten dollars a pair. In 1909 California put its Hayward Game Farm into production. The Yountville Game Farm was in production by 1926 and during the next twenty-eight years more than a million artificially reared pheasants went from these enclosures to all parts of California, but became established only in the fertile valleys with diversified farming, including grain production, especially the rice farming areas. Nearly half of California's annual hunting season kill of a half million pheasants came from the Sacramento Valley.

Michigan established its first game farm in 1917. There had been sporadic planting of pheasants by individual private citizens before that. In Holland, Michigan, A. G. Baumgartel turned loose a few birds in March 1894, perhaps the first pheasants in Michigan. One brood was seen. No more. But following the regular stocking from the game farm in 1917, pheasants increased rapidly and Michigan had its first open hunting season for them within eight years.

South Dakota, which now classifies itself as the "top pheasant state in the nation," usually has a season kill of more than 3,000,000 ringnecks. The average hunter takes twenty birds each season, as compared with 4.5 birds per hunter in the next best state. Yet South Dakota acquired its fantastic pheasant population at only slight expense. It is the kind of Horatio Alger story that encouraged less favored states to waste great sums hopefully rearing and stocking pheasants. South Dakota never did operate a game farm.

Before 1890 South Dakota had to plug along as best it could with only its native game birds, the bobwhite quail and the prairie chicken, plus ducks and geese. During the three decades from 1870 to 1900 market hunters ranged through the state plundering whatever they could peddle. Typical was a story in the Black Hills *Journal* four days before Christmas, 1883. "Some parties brought a load of grouse to town yesterday," said the news item. "They disposed of them readily at a good price." The same paper reported on the same day that "Americus Thomson arrived in town from the Moreau River Wednesday with a wagonload of game. He reports buffalo very scarce, and his load was made up principally of antelope."

During those years when the game resources were being reduced at a staggering pace eastern South Dakota was within the "chicken country." It might have been in part the abrupt reduction of the native game birds that prompted residents to turn to foreign species to fill the gap.

In 1891 N. L. Witcher, according to an old newspaper account, announced that he was having shipped into Sturgis, South Dakota, some pheasants from Oregon. He would appreciate it if everyone would leave them alone so they might prosper. He pointed out that they were prolific and hardy, and he anticipated that, given a little protection for a few years, the pheasants would ". . . drive out the vulgar native grouse, which are not really game birds. . . ."

It may be, however, that Witcher's long-tailed Oriental chickens never did reach Sturgis. No one has ever recorded a further mention of them. If these birds did not arrive to "drive out the vulgar native grouse," the honor of being the original members of their species to take up residence in South Dakota goes to pheasants introduced by Dr. A. Zetlitz, who lived in Sioux Falls. In 1898 he had several pairs of pheasants shipped in from Illinois. When the pheasants, which numbered half a dozen ringnecks, plus a few assorted golden and silver pheasants, reached Sioux Falls, the doctor deposited them in cages along with his collection of peacocks, wood ducks, and Canadian geese.

Dr. Zetlitz, however, from the first, was determined to turn out any surplus pheasants he might rear. The next spring he released ten pheasants in Minnehaha County. For a few years the birds were reported from widely scattered regions; then they disappeared. But the doctor turned loose some more in 1903 and these apparently enjoyed better fortune. Other private individuals stocked some more pheasants during the following years, as they were doing in many parts of the country in that period.

In 1911 the state bought 200 pairs from a game farm and displayed them at the state fair. They were offered in groups of three hens and a cock to curious and eager farmers along the James River. Now the ringnecked pheasant was really launched in what would become one of its strongholds on the North American continent.

So well did the birds prosper that the state was able to discontinue its major stocking efforts in 1917 after turning out a total of only 7000 pheasants. South Dakota held its first open season in 1919, and within another five or six years its fantastic pheasant hunting was attracting national attention. The start in pheasants had cost South Dakota $20,000. Other less fortunate states were to go on seeing their investment in the birds skyrocket year after year as they hopefully bolstered pheasant populations with annual plantings.

By 1941 J. W. Cluett, director of South Dakota's Department of Game, Fish and Parks, was able to make some striking statements in a booklet whose very title, *50 Million Pheasants in South Dakota*, must have stirred envy in the hearts of Chamber of Commerce employees in other regions.

"It has been estimated," wrote Director Cluett, "that since the first open season in 1919 (to 1940) approximately

20,000,000 pheasants have been *legally* killed in South Dakota." He computed this to be the equivalent of more than 3000 carloads of beef. At that time hunters were taking a million and a half pheasants each season, without reducing the birds' ability to bring their numbers back the following year. "For a period of 15 to 60 days," he added, "the fields and byroads of the State re-echo to a barrage of shotgun fire and the rattle of some 350,000 pounds of birdshot against the cornstalks. . . ."

The pheasant became the state's most popular bird. Consequently, in the 1943 session of the South Dakota State Legislature, the alien white man designated the alien pheasant as the "state bird," an honor it promises to retain indefinitely.

According to an official history of the Department of Game, Fish and Parks, written by Don Hipschman, "Nearly every South Dakota town east of the Missouri River and a few west of the Missouri advertise themselves as 'The Pheasant Capital of the world.'" The pheasant brought so many visiting hunters and so much money to the state that the Department of Game, Fish and Parks, at the end of the 1946 fiscal year, found itself with a $3,000,000 balance in the bank, a rare situation indeed for a state conservation agency in a state as thinly populated as South Dakota is.

Nebraska, also one of the best pheasant-producing states today, also began in a small way. From only 1000 pheasants originally brought to the state, technicians live-trapped and transplanted 40,000 descendants within a few years.

If you look at a map of the western end of Lake Erie you will see Pelee Island. Part of the providence of Ontario, Canada, it lies off Point Pelee, separated from Ohio by twenty miles of often turbulent lake water, and it is only seven miles long and half as wide. Until pheasants came along, it attracted scant attention from the mainland.

According to the late Frank Vorhees, a long-time employee of the Ohio Division of Conservation, the ringneck got his start there as part of a hush-hush wildlife swap. Vorhees once described the episode in detail.

Ontario biologists wanted pheasants for Pelee Island about the time Ohio fisheries people were searching for a stock of bass to bring in for fish hatchery experimental work. The deal, according to Vorhees, was to swap 100 bass for 100 pheasants. Vorhees, a game warden at the time, was assigned to take the pheasants to Pelee Island and bring the bass back with him. "I didn't know where Pelee Island was," he said, "I'd never even heard of the place."

Ohio officials, worried about repercussions if the state's hunters heard of this scheme to export some of their prized pheasants, instructed Vorhees to keep the whole thing quiet.

At the Wellington Game Farm he picked up two crates of half-grown pheasants. With his birds on the back seat, Vorhees turned his Model-T north toward Lake Erie where he met a co-worker who manned a fast little boat in the service of the state. On Pelee Island they were met at the dock by Frank Barnes, driving an old market wagon drawn by an aging gray horse. "While Frank drove around the island," Vorhees reported, "I stood in the wagon bed and tossed out pheasants—two at a time." The passage of the creaking wagon was hardly noted in the farmhouses along the dirt roads.

All the way back across Lake Erie, Vorhees dipped up fresh lake water for the bass which made the trip in four milk cans. "I didn't lose a pheasant going over," he said proudly, "nor a fish coming back."

Vorhees almost forgot about the birds he had taken across Lake Erie, until several years later he received a letter from Toronto. Officials there had learned that the original pheasants were brought to Pelee Island by a Frank Vorhees. Was he the same man? If so, would he like to come back and sample the pheasant hunting? Vorhees did go back. "If I hadn't seen it," he said, "I wouldn't have believed it. There were pheasants everywhere. You had to get out and chase them out of the road." Farm people, who at first destroyed pheasant nests to save their grain, learned that the pheasant was a major economic asset. Islanders now rent rooms and provide meals for thousands of hunters during the brief but profitable fall pheasant hunts.

Why did the pheasants prosper so on their island in the lake and usually maintain their fall populations at the amazing level of five birds per acre? According to Dr. Allen W. Stokes, who made extensive studies of Pelee Island pheasants, there were at least five factors contributing to their success. The pheasants have good supplies of food throughout the year and good cover, especially during the nesting season. They are seldom disturbed by mowing machines because there is little livestock farming on Pelee, and consequently not much hay is grown. The winters are relatively mild. And predators are rare on the island. But there is also the fact that the young pheasants, even when hatched into a world already crowded with their kind, have no place else to go. Frank Vorhees' unheralded journey across Lake Erie produced a fantastic success story for the big game bird.

Today the pheasant has been moved to every part of the country where it might have the ghost of a chance for survival, as well as many areas where it had no chance at all. Two-thirds of a century after Owen Denny's historic haphazard experiment, those areas of the country where the ringneck could perpetuate himself were firmly established. Some states struck it rich; they were fitted by nature and land use to the needs of the bird. Pheasant fanciers elsewhere never knew until they tried that they were destined for failure. And then it was often hard for them to believe. Consequently, great sums have been wasted in efforts to establish this bird where conditions were not right for its success.

Most frustrated of all those who have tried and failed are perhaps the wildlife technicians in the southeastern states. In that section of the country the pheasant has consistently refused to establish permanent breeding populations. Hundreds of thousands of dollars have been expended in pursuit of this elusive goal. As late as the 1950s the state of Kentucky released 20,000 ringnecks in an eight-year program.

What are the factors that make living intolerable for the pheasant in these southeastern states? As early as 1930 Aldo Leopold noted that the southern limits of the pheasant range matched closely the southern limits of the last of the great glaciers. He believed there might be a relationship between calcium content of the topsoil and pheasant egg hatchability. Later, controlled experiments did indicate that calcium-deficient diets in breeding pheasants reduced reproductive success.

Others thought the higher temperature on the eggs during the pre-incubation period might cut down on the hatching success. This, too, was checked out experimentally. Higher temperatures did, as was suspected, reduce hatchability.

But what of the exceptions? What about the high temperature in the Imperial Valley of California where pheasants had established breeding populations? There the climate was dry, while in the southeastern states it was humid. To this day the real combination of limiting factors determining the successful breeding range of the ringneck in this country is not well understood. There may, it is believed, be factors at work which biologists have not yet suspected. Until the answers are known, and all possibilities explored, hope will not die completely for the ringneck down south.

Meanwhile, efforts have been turned to other races of pheasants that might be better adapted to those areas having warm, humid climates and low levels of soil fertility. The native range of pheasants covers a wide variety of climates and terrain across southern and Central Asia from Asia Minor to eastern China and Korea.

Researchers have experimented with various hybrid and crossbred combinations of pheasants. Pheasants of different varieties are so closely related that such crosses produce fertile eggs. And this promises all manner of possibilities in fitting various strains of pheasants to territories where their relatives have never succeeded. So, hopefully, the perpetual search goes on, with each new group of pheasant transplanters seeing blue sky and rainbows because they go about this work more scientifically than did some of their predecessors.

In sportsman's clubs and barber shops, and not a few game and fish departments, the well of hope never runs dry. "If we could," they sigh, "just have it like they got it in South Dakota." The truth, fortunate or unfortunate, is that in most places they can't have it "like they got it in South Dakota," because they cannot change either the climate or the soil type. Nor can they easily or quickly change the pattern of their agriculture. And all of these, plus the genetics of the bird, are important factors determining the pheasant's welfare.

The pheasant and its regional success has encouraged people to search for other foreign species of game animals when they might better have spent their time and money improving habitat for native species. Those students prompted to question the wisdom of such transplanting programs are invariably advised to "look at the pheasant."

The pheasant is a fine bird, and a joy to hunt, a pleasure to eat and an economic asset to much of the country. But he was ushered into this hemisphere with no more scientific study or biological awareness than were a host of other foreign wild creatures.

Consequently we must in fairness look not alone at the pheasant. We must also look at the house sparrow, look at the carp, and look at the European starling. In each we trusted to luck, which comes in two varieties, good and bad. As with a game of Russian roulette, men took a chance. And having committed the act we can blame no one else for the bad luck because we asked for it. In the areas where the pheasant succeeded, it was good luck—and little else.

While the ringneck stands as the grand exhibit of the animal transplanters, two other game birds hold regional runner-up positions. One is the Hungarian partridge, a wild chicken with short wings, a stubby tail, and over-all about twice the size of a bobwhite quail. This bird traces its ancestry to Europe and northern Asia. The partridge is considered a notable success in the farming regions of the prairie provinces and a few north-central states where it has become an important game bird at a surprisingly low investment.

In 1908 Fred J. Green released in the grain fields near Calgary, Alberta, seven pairs of Hungarian partridges live-trapped and shipped directly from Hungary. The following year, drawing on some $3000 donated by enthusiastic sportsmen, Green had another ninety-five pairs shipped in to supplement the original release. The only additional release was in 1914, when ten pairs were turned out.

Gradually, as the transplanters worked with the Hungarian partridge over the years, a few facts became increasingly clear. They learned that this bird would thrive only in the fertile agricultural regions where small grains provided it suitable food and cover. Calgary happened to be the heart of such an area. Such northern states as North Dakota, Montana, and Minnesota also proved suitable for it. But the Hungarian partridge was slowly drawing its own lines. Where the environment did not meet its needs it quickly disappeared, and no amount of hopeful replenishing of the dwindling stock would alter the course.

These birds so appealed to American sportsmen that they were released in at least forty-two states and have been turned out repeatedly in places where they failed to fit into the wild community. During 1908 and 1909 importers brought 40,000 of them into the United States. Illinois tried 6000 pairs of them and Indiana spent $62,208 on them between 1889 and 1912. Connecticut tried 1400 of them without tasting success, and Michigan turned out 10,000 that disappeared.

Pennsylvania game managers began stocking them seriously in 1926. In the following fifteen years they released 31,000 wild-trapped, plus 2000 pen-reared partridges at a total cost of $131,000. Recently M. J. Golden, executive director of the Pennsylvania Game Commission, said, "There have been no reports of Hungarian partridges in Pennsylvania for a number of years." And the failures have been repeated in numerous other states.

The next runner-up, the chukar partridge from India, was attracting more and more interest. The first of these birds given their freedom in North America were perhaps five pairs shipped to Illinois from Karachi, India, in 1893. Nova Scotia and Massachusetts also received early shipments. But not until the 1930s was the bird given a full trial in the United States.

The chukar is a handsome bird of grayish-blue plumage, with heavily barred markings on his sides and a dark band that extends from the base of the beak, through the eyes, and down the side of the neck and around to the throat. Males weigh an average one pound and four ounces.

One of the first states to take the chukar seriously was Missouri, which in 1934 obtained five of the birds from California. Three years later there were a thousand of them in the game-farm pens. Missouri biologists, however, held no great hope for the bird. They had checked the nature of the mountainous terrain of Nepal, where the birds lived naturally, and saw scant resemblance between it and the Missouri countryside. They were not greatly surprised when the released birds failed to become established.

Pennsylvania released sixty-eight of the birds in the northwestern part of the state in 1936. In the next few years they turned out nearly 2000 additional chukars. Said Richard Gerstell of the Pennsylvania Game Commission before the fifth North American Wildlife Conference in 1940, "As a general rule, regardless of the time and place of release, the birds [chukars] shortly dispersed in all directions, completely vanishing within a period of a few weeks."

One lone chukar joined a flock of free-ranging Pennsylvania domestic turkeys and, like a mascot, trailed the great native American birds on their daytime foraging and roosted with them at night. Wildlife biologists, sensing that the bird might have discovered its niche in the Pennsylvania landscape, brought it the company of forty more chukars. A week later the forty late arrivals had disappeared—and with them had gone the chukar who lived with the turkeys.

Finally, and sadly, Pennsylvania gave the chukar up as a bad risk. So did Minnesota, which released an estimated 85,-000 of the birds.

But in the arid Great Basin the chukar story was taking a different turn. These rocky, barren-looking hillsides with their sparse stand of sage seem not to discourage the chukars so long as the birds can find water. Today Nevada calls the chukar its number-one upland game bird. Washington, Utah, Idaho, California, Oregon, Wyoming, and Montana have sizable chukar partridge populations.

Together these three foreigners, the ringneck pheasant, Hungarian partridge, and chukar partridge, comprise the strongest arguments favoring continued efforts to establish exotic newcomers in the United States.

Chapter 4

Brown Trout's Travels

THE Rio Calcurrupe, tumbling down cold and clear between two ranges of timbered mountains in Central Chile, is one of the world's finest trout-fishing streams. This is a stream neither easily reached nor leisurely waded in traditional trout-fishing fashion. It is a brawling, rumbling little river through much of its length, and those who are privileged to fish it do so from wooden boats carried by the current and maneuvered by expert boatmen.

To reach the Calcurrupe you venture to the self-sufficient mountain village of Llifen. Here the people still make their own shoes, mill their own flour, and provide many of their other needs ranging from building materials to wine. In the dirt street the ox carts creak along on wheels of solid wood, and the goat herdsman follows his flock past the old frame hotel twice a day on the way to pasture and back.

You ride up the valley in the morning on an aging flat-bed truck loaded with boats, guides, and lunch. You float downstream and come out in the evening within a couple of miles of Llifen. On the average day you will probably be carrying several ten- to twelve-pound brown and rainbow trout and will have released several others. If you have caught a twenty-pound trout, the local people will smile and nod appreciatively, but they know this is not unusual—not on the Calcurrupe, blessed as it is with its great imported cold-water fish.

Cousins of the trout in the Calcurrupe have now been transported to widely separated waters around the world. Brown trout grow in the streams and lakes of New Zealand as well as in some of the more favored waters of North America. The brown trout, like the ringneck pheasant, is a creature to which the animal movers point with pride. And who can find fault with a ten-pound trout?

Nature originally limited this wary, heavy-bodied trout to the waters of Europe, Algeria, and a corner of Asia. But in the mid 1800s Europeans settling new parts of the world wanted to take their favorite trout with them. This was the beginning of the successful travels of the brown trout.

Here is a handsome fish. His back shades from olive and greenish brown into yellows along the sides and finally to gray or white on the belly. The back and sides are also decorated with large dark spots. In November and December in the Northern Hemisphere the females move up the streams and deposit their eggs in saucer-shaped nests cleaned out in the gravel beds. Depending on her size and age, the female may lay from 200 to 6000 eggs, and these, providing the water remains at a constant temperature of 51 degrees F., hatch in forty-eight to fifty-two days.

How big will brown trout get? They mature in three or four years and average four to seven pounds by the sixth year. Weights of eight to twelve pounds are not uncommon and in 1937 a net took one of 37¾ pounds from an impoundment of the Logan River in Utah. The world's record brown trout taken on hook and line is a fish taken in Scotland in 1866; it weighed 39½ pounds.

It is a far simpler matter to catch a rainbow than a wary brown trout. Cautious and knowledgeable anglers applying every bit of their skill find a match in the brown, and this challenge alone endears the fish to the seasoned fly-rod fisherman.

Consequently, as early as 1851, brown trout eggs were being meticulously crated, iced, and hopefully shipped out to

Tasmania from England. But storms, lack of experience, and shortages of ice usually plagued these early efforts. Then in 1864 one shipment of brown trout eggs carried on the steamer *Norfolk* did make it after ninety-one days at sea. And, as the story goes, the trout eggs were escorted from the harbor by a brass band. In the Tasmanian hatchery 300 of the eggs hatched. Here was the beginning stock for brown trout that would eventually be shipped to Australia and New Zealand.

In the same year that Tasmania received its first brown trout eggs, another shipment was sent out to New Zealand. But, as was so often the case, these fish were doomed. Six hundred of them were put aboard the *British Empire* destined for A. M. Johnson in Christchurch. All of them died within minutes of each other. Later a lump of white-lead putty was found on the bottom of the container where a careless deckhand had dropped it.

Now Johnson turned to Tasmania where the browns were becoming well established. He purchased 800 eggs. To Johnson's sorrow, only three of the eggs hatched. But three fish were better than none, assuming of course that they were not all of the same sex. Next one of the little trout escaped and was lost. The remaining two were installed in a pond in the gardens maintained by the Canterbury Acclimatization Society. Then, according to records of the society, "A tremendous flood, the highest ever known in Canterbury, submerged the Gardens, and although most of the stock was saved, the trout were washed out into a swamp leading to the river, and appeared hopelessly lost." But the undaunted trout fanciers had built a spawning enclosure before the flood, and the only two brown trout believed to exist in all of New Zealand were found in the new raceway. Now, as if to prove the value of faith and persistence, these fish turned out to be male and female.

For the next several years these two brown trout yielded an annual supply of ova to the club, and within a few years the society was selling young trout to other groups and individuals in many parts of New Zealand, and all the while releasing brown trout by the thousands into near-by rivers and lakes. From these original two fish, plus a few other shipments that followed from Tasmania, have come the brown trout that brought New Zealand her reputation as one of the finest places in the world for trout fishing.

When first turned out in New Zealand waters, the brown trout grew at impressive speed to sizes that amazed the fish culturists. One investigator of the time computed the rate of growth in Otago streams, between 1878 and 1883, at 1.53 pounds per fish annually. In some waters they were said to add three and a half pounds in a single year. Brown trout fry liberated in the Shag River in 1868 were caught four years later at weights of more than fourteen pounds, while one female trout was said to have grown to sixteen and a half pounds in this period.

In spite of the fact that fishermen in New Zealand, as everywhere, are seldom inclined to shrink a fish, the brown trout apparently did grow at prodigious rates. Conditions were nearly ideal. Competition from other fish was light and insects and crustaceans provided abundant food. Their growth rate gradually declined, however, according to those who worked with the brown trout in those years. Why? Some people blamed the growing horde of foreign birds being introduced into New Zealand about that time and speculated that the imported birds were stealing grasshoppers and flies from the imported trout.

Almost two decades passed following establishment of brown trout in New Zealand before they were successfully brought to North America. Then Herr Von Behr, president of the *Deutsche Fischerei Verein*, sent a shipment of eggs across the North Atlantic during the winter of 1882–83. When they reached the Northville Hatchery in New York on February 18, 1883, state hatchery superintendent Fred Mather took charge of them.

In spite of the fact that some local trout fishermen considered the brown trout a rough fish, fry were released the following April in Michigan's Père Marquette River.

Meanwhile, Herr Von Behr sent 40,000 more eggs to Mather early in 1885. From these came 28,000 fry, most destined for the waters of Long Island near the Hudson.

By this time another development was confusing the picture of the brown trout in America. The year following Von Behr's initial shipment, Fred Mather took steps to acquire stock of the Loch Leven trout directly from Scotland and set the stage for an argument that would go on for years among trout fanciers and fish culturists in this country.

Preparation of the first shipment from Scotland began on a November day at the Howietun Fish Hatchery on the shore of Loch Leven. Loch Leven is an unimpressive shallow lake believed once to have been connected with the sea. The fish culturists collected 120,000 eggs from the eight-year old breeders in the hatchery raceways. They spread the eggs out gently on squares of muslin with 950 eggs to the layer. Three of these layers were then arranged in a tray and the trays packed into a case. On top of the case went a tray of ice packed in moss and sawdust. When the shipment was ready, six of these trout egg cases held the precious shipment.

It was only an hour's run down to the harbor at Glasgow, and there the half-dozen cases of trout eggs were loaded aboard the steamship *Furnessia,* about to depart for the United States. The Scottish hatcherymen believed that ice would delay the hatching until the first week of February.

Carrying the cases of trout eggs in her ice room, the *Furnessia* docked in New York on New Year's Day, 1885. Meanwhile, Fred Mather up at the state fish hatchery had been waiting impatiently for the eggs. Mather cleared the shipment through customs the day after New Year's and at eight o'clock in the evening of January 2, 1885, arrived with them at the Cold Spring Harbor Hatchery on Long Island.

Mather was so impressed with the efficiency of the egg

crates that he used them a few days later to ship whitefish eggs to Germany and Switzerland. Then, on January 5, Mather sent the first 10,000 trout eggs from Scotland off to General R. U. Sherman, then a member of the New York State Fish Commission, and also president of a trout club at Wilmurt, New York, in the Adirondacks. On January 29, 5000 of the brown trout eggs from Loch Leven went out from Northville to E. B. Hodge at Plymouth, New Hampshire. Hodge planted them in Sunapee Lake and wrote back that he had lost only 118. Another 20,000 eggs went to Anamosa, Iowa, and fry from them were turned out in West Okoboji Lake. St. Paul, Minnesota, received 20,000 eggs. Freezing weather killed 3000 of 10,000 eggs sent to Maine, and those that did hatch were turned out in Branch Pond at Ellsworth.

The rest of the eggs were retained at the Northville hatchery and the fry were shipped out of there for other points between April 10 and 23. In that period, 10,000 brown trout fry went to the Michigan Fish Commission, 5000 to L. S. Hill at Grand Rapids, Michigan, 1500 to G. H. Dalrymple also of Grand Rapids, and 20,000 to the Crooked Lake hatchery in northern Michigan. The final 7000 fry were kept in the hatchery at Northville. Thus, the first big successful shipment of brown trout to this country was now successfully distributed to widely separated geographical locations.

By this time there was much discussion about the two kinds of brown trout. Some people considered them separate species and spoke of the German brown trout and the Loch Leven trout. But in due time scientists determined that trout from both sources were of the same species and ceased to worry much about where they had originated.

Today brown trout live as permanent residents in most of the streams of the United States cold enough and clean enough to support them. Outside this range brown trout are frequently stocked by the tens of thousands on a dump-and-catch plan without hope that they will establish breeding populations.

You can, however, find many an angler willing to curse the day brown trout were first imported. Some dislike them because they destroy rainbow and brook trout. Some dislike them for the same traits that have brought them approval in other quarters—their ability to avoid being caught. In British Columbia, where the brown trout was first introduced between 1932 and 1935 to satisfy the demands of anglers, these European trout have now become firmly established. "While brown trout have apparently succeeded in becoming established," say G. Clifford Carl and C. J. Guiguet in the British Columbia Provincial Museum Handbook No. 14, "they have not proved to be entirely satisfactory. Although they are present the year around, they are more difficult to catch than are the native species and are less attractive to the average angler."

But the brown trout's defenders outnumber his detractors and class him with the ringneck pheasant as one of the rare exceptions to the record of failures scored by those who mix up the world's wildlife.

Chapter 5

Marine Fish That Moved

In his official duty as chairman of the California Fish Commission, S. R. Throckmorton looked long and critically at the list of salt-water fish with which the Almighty had blessed the West Coast of the United States. When compared with the species living along the Atlantic coast, it became apparent to Commissioner Throckmorton that his state of California had been slighted. If there was a single fish that he most envied the East Coast citizens, it was the magnificent, strong striped bass, *Roccus saxatilis,* known in some parts of its range as "rockfish," or just "rock." As Throckmorton reviewed the situation, he saw one recent development that might now make it possible to transplant the striped bass: railroads had recently spanned the continent.

Preliminary arrangements were soon made with friends in the East, and in 1897 a train arrived in San Francisco carrying as part of its freight a tank of yearling striped bass that had traveled all the way from New Jersey. They were released in San Francisco Bay. Two years later a second planting of striped bass was brought from the East Coast to reinforce them. The total was 435 fish.

Throckmorton had been right. The Pacific coast was suited to the striped bass. They multiplied with fantastic speed. Within a single decade following their first release, striped bass were being sold in large quantites at the fish markets in San Francisco. Within twenty years, according to the records of the U. S. Bureau of Fisheries, the commercial catch had climbed to 1,234,000 pounds a year. In 1915, the year of the biggest catch, commercial fishermen brought one and three-quarter million pounds of them to market.

By now these large commercial hauls were being viewed with alarm among sport fishermen along the West Coast. In 1935 they had succeeded in removing the striped bass from the fish markets and elevating it to the rank of a protected game fish.

Today stripers are considered the primary game fish of the Sacramento-San Joaquin Delta. Here in the San Francisco Bay area they have reached their greatest abundance, at a latitude corresponding to their area of peak abundance back on their original East Coast territory. Meanwhile, they have continued to spread in smaller numbers southward to Los Angeles, and north as far as the Columbia River on the Washington-Oregon border. Understandably, California has never viewed this introduced fish as anything less than a blessing.

One reason anglers appreciate this fish is its size. Twelve, fifteen, and twenty pounders are common along the Atlantic coast, while a fifty or sixty pounder is always a possibility. The biggest one ever taken by hook and line was dragged in from the surf at Vineyard Sound, Massachusetts, in August 1913 by Charles B. Church. It was five feet long and weighed seventy-three pounds.

The striped bass, however, has more than size to recommend him. He is heavily muscled and strong of spirit. He tests the full measure of skill, strength, and nerve of any angler whose artificial spoon or jig he happens to mistake for a swimming bait fish. The pounding surf that beats the seawater into an unsteady froth holds no fear for the striped bass. He dashes through the waves under full control and pursues his food with reckless abandon. Year after year he lures hundreds of thousands of fishermen to the ocean.

This fish has a white belly that darkens gradually along his

sides until he is green or greenish-blue above. Six or seven
rows of dark spots extend from the back of the gill cover to
the base of his tail. By the time he is three, the male is sexually
mature, and by now his length exceeds ten inches. The female, meanwhile, matures when she is closer to seventeen or
eighteen inches and more than four years old.

It has been estimated that a seventy-five-pound female
could drop as many as 10,000,000 eggs in a single spawning
season. One of twelve pounds has been known to produce a
million and a quarter eggs. Each of the tiny eggs is but a
twentieth of an inch in diameter and they sink so slowly that
if the water has the slightest current they are likely to drift
and float continuously until they hatch, a ride that lasts
seventy-four hours in fifty-eight-degree water and forty-
eight hours when the water is sixty-seven degrees. The
specific gravity of the eggs makes them slightly heavier than
fresh water, and in still water they slowly settle to the bottom where they may become covered with silt and die. The
young fish stay in the rivers and brackish estuaries, wandering
and feeding until they are nearly two years old. Then, as
tagging studies have shown, they congregate in large schools
and make lengthy migrations.

Any fish or shellfish they can catch and consume is fair
game to the striped bass. Herring, menhaden, shad, smelt,
crabs, shrimp, and mussels become their easy prey. In the
spring the adults move into the fresh waters of the spawning streams and back out again in late summer and early fall.
Unlike some species, they do not go far to sea but spend
their time instead near the mouths of the rivers or in the
deeper, weedy waters along the islands and ledges. The
striped bass frequently leads a long life. One of them kept
in the New York Aquarium lived to be twenty-three years
old.

Along its native Atlantic coast the striped bass ranges all
the way from Cape Breton Island, Nova Scotia, south to
Florida. The spawning area extends largely from New

Jersey to South Carolina. During the spawning seasons striped bass leave their salt-water habitat and move up the coastal streams to drop their eggs. On occasion the creation of new dams across their spawning streams has interrupted their age-old routine. When this happened on the Cooper River, which flows down out of Central South Carolina to enter the ocean at Charleston, it did more than cut off the migration path of the striped bass; it led to speculation among alert fisheries biologists that the future for this fish might hold even more fantastic travels than his historic trip from New Jersey to California.

This phase of the striped-bass travelogue began on a day in November 1941 when engineers closed the gates in the new Pinopolis Dam at Moncks Corner, South Carolina. Waters that backed up behind the dam formed the Santee-Cooper Reservoir covering 160,000 acres. The reservoir is actually composed of two lakes connected by a canal. Lake Marion covers 100,000 acres and Lake Moultrie 60,000. The canal diverts the waters of the Santee River down the Cooper River to the ocean. "The primary purpose of the reservoir," says South Carolina fisheries biologist Robert E. Stevens, "is electrical power which is generated at Pinopolis Dam on Lake Moultrie." Also at Pinopolis Dam is a navigation lock which is 180 feet long, sixty feet wide and has a lift of seventy-five feet."

"Historically," says Stevens, "a seasonal run of striped bass . . . occurred in both the Santee and Cooper Rivers." No one was much surprised to find striped bass in the tailwaters below the new Pinopolis Dam, and even the isolated catches which soon began to occur in the new reservoir did not arouse much speculation. It was, after all, quite logical that the gates on the dam would lock some striped bass inside the reservoir.

Within a few years, however, fishermen began to notice young stripers schooling in the new lakes, fish that were obviously younger than the dam. Biologists, aware that the navigation locks in the Pinopolis Dam were frequently opened for the passage of boats, could never say for certain that these young rockfish had not been locked through with the river traffic. But it began to appear that the rockfish might now be completing their entire life cycle in the impoundments. If true, this opened whole new horizons to fish managers. Was it possible that the striped bass could actually thrive in fresh water throughout its life, perhaps in lakes as far inland as those of Arkansas, Kentucky, or Oklahoma?

Within a few years following the completion of Lakes Marion and Moultrie, the striped bass were well along on a population explosion. Fishing there for the big bass became famous. Word spread through angling circles across the country. The quality of this fishing has since fallen off drastically. Striped bass are still there in good numbers, but they are no longer as easily caught as they once were.

All this sudden striped-bass bonanza was duly reported by South Carolina fisheries biologists in the 1950s during meetings of professional groups such as the Southeastern Association of Game and Fish Commissioners. Soon biologists from a dozen states had visions of rockfish dancing through their minds.

One of these was Andrew Hulsey, the highly respected youthful chief of the Arkansas Division of Fisheries. Arkansas at the time was, as Hulsey said later, ". . . knocking itself out trying to attract tourist business and part of our campaign was trying hard to have the best fishing in the United States." Hulsey was alert for any fish that offered a combination of huge trophy size, fast growth, and hard fighting qualities, all of which it began to appear were possessed by the glamorous striped bass.

Meanwhile, if anyone still had serious doubt over whether or not these fish might actually be able to live the year round in fresh water, the proof was not long in coming. In 1953 the Roanoke River was dammed to form a sprawling thirty-nine mile-long impoundment on the Virginia-North Carolina border. This lake, with its 800 miles of shoreline, was called Kerr Reservoir, and, like the dam at Moncks Corner, it stood in the historic path of migrating striped bass. But unlike the lake in South Carolina, Kerr Reservoir had no navigation locks.

From its fish hatchery at Weldon, North Carolina obtained 1,000,000 tiny striped bass in the spring of 1953 and released them above the dam in the new Kerr Reservoir. One way or another they were going to find out whether this fish really could be produced in fresh water. The following year they planted a million more young rockfish in the lake, and they followed up with still a third million in 1955. Then they stopped and waited.

In the summer of 1956 an angler took a small striped bass from Kerr Reservoir. Fisheries biologists studying the little bass determined that it had hatched one year after they had put the final stock in the lake. "The presence of this one fish," however, said the cautious fisheries biologists, "could not be taken as positive proof of natural reproduction— but it opens possibilities."

As time wore on, more young fish were taken from Kerr. And in following years it was definitely established that this lake, completely landlocked from salt water, had populations of striped bass living from egg to maturity.

Now the striper stampede was on. Other states began thinking about their own lakes that might suit this big strong fish. In Kentucky, biologists thought Kentucky Lake and Lake Cumberland might be ideal. Tennessee, Oklahoma, Texas, Georgia, and Arkansas were eagerly considering their lakes.

In November of 1956, Andy Hulsey had already dispatched two Arkansas technicians to Moncks Corner to catch a load of striped bass. Then they were to arrange air transport to get the fish back to the hills of Arkansas. Because there was no plane available for the flight, the two fisheries workers loaded their fish, all of which were from two to ten inches long, into barrels and put them on their truck. Then they started the long haul back across the mid-South. When they arrived, weary and sleepless, a saddened group of fisheries workers found that a fungus disease had killed every one of the striped bass.

Next they returned to South Carolina and caught 207 striped bass in a variety of sizes. They managed to get all these back to Arkansas alive and gently placed twenty-seven of the biggest ones in Lake Ouachita, a timber-rimmed impoundment that reaches up a thousand wild hollows in the oak- and hickory-covered Ouachita Mountains. In four years the determined Arkansas crews caught and released 1148 striped bass, mostly in the same lake. One load of thirty-five were turned out in Lake Greeson early in the project.

In spite of the fact that Arkansas technicians have not collected encouraging evidence of established populations in either lake, they still live in hope.

Meanwhile, Kentucky technicians joined forces with those from neighboring Tennessee to attempt planting the striped bass in the 186-mile long Kentucky Lake, first and biggest of the TVA impoundments. Then in 1957 they released twelve fish, of two to twelve pounds each, from Moncks Corner into the 101-mile long Lake Cumberland in the mountainous section of eastern Kentucky. In theory either of these lakes might have provided conditions needed for the success of the striped bass.

Now the foremost question was whether or not the imported stripers would reproduce in this land of race horses and bourbon. In an effort to recover some of the minute eggs, if indeed any existed, Dr. Hunter Hancock, limnologist at Kentucky State Teachers College, was assigned in the spring of 1960 to go to the mouth of the Dix River with extremely small mesh nets. On hand also were observers from several near-by states. The net collected twenty-four eggs that looked as though they might, in fact, have been dropped by striped bass. The eggs were sent off hopefully to Dr.

Romeo Mansueti, an expert on striped bass at the Chesapeake Biological Laboratory at Solomons, Maryland. There was, Dr. Mansueti said, no question about it; these were rockfish eggs—but they were dead eggs.

The following spring the egg hunters returned to the mouth of the Dix. This time they discovered a few living eggs. But there the Kentucky version of the striped-bass story stands. No one knows for certain what lies ahead for the striped bass in Kentucky. After several years' effort the technicians are still "hopefully optimistic."

So far striped bass have not prospered far from salt water, and the fish planters still search hopefully for proof that it can reproduce inland as it has in Kerr Reservoir and Santee-Cooper.

There have been other efforts to install this fish in new waters and most likely the travels of the striped bass are not completed yet. The vision of a silvery-sided sixty-pound fish of great strength is a powerful motivating force among people not content with such magnificent native species as the largemouth, smallmouth, and spotted black bass. As long as hope survives that the striped bass may become adapted to a full life span in fresh water, moving day will be imminent for *Roccus saxatilis*.

Chapter 6

Where the Pigs Run Wild

―――――❦―――――

In the tangled depths of the laurel thickets far up the rocky-timbered slopes of the Great Smoky Mountains lives a thriving band of wild Russian hogs famous for their evil temper and their ability to rip open a hound dog or drive a mountain man up an ash tree. When these wild hogs came to the Smokies, the native wildlife had little choice but to move over and give them room. In addition to the acorns and roots which form his dietary staples, reptiles, mammals, birds, and amphibians go to fatten the hog. The eggs of the wild turkey and the grouse attract his attention.

Meanwhile, the white man—the other dominant exotic now well established in these hills and hollows himself—spread tales, true and false, about the squinty-eyed wild swine. The "Roosians" traits became legendary throughout that mountainous region where Tennessee and North Carolina come together.

Most people would agree that the wild European boar added nothing of beauty to these haze-shrouded hills. He stands high at the shoulders and, bison-like, slopes off toward his rear quarters. He has a short tail with a brush on the end, and his coarse dark coat bristles with silvery guard hairs. Beneath it all he wears a thick-growing undercoat of heavy wool.

Wild boars are known to attain weights of 400 pounds and more, although average weights reached by those in the

Smokies are believed to be considerably below this. A wild boar of 225 pounds is considered large.

A typical boar has a long, knobby, wedge-shaped snout. His tusks may grow to be eight inches long and his upper canines curve, not downward but upward, and equip him with sharp-pointed bone hooks with which he can tear up roots or disembowel an enemy. The lower canines grind constantly against the upper ones as the hogs feed. This keeps the tusks razor sharp. As fast as the canine teeth are worn down, they grow fresh from the root.

According to wildlife biologist Perry Jones, who studied the wild boars for the North Carolina Wildlife Resources Commission, "The imported boars seem particularly to relish rattlesnakes, which they kill with their sharp-edge hoofs." They will, according to still another observer, walk right up to a coiled rattler and, ". . . literally eat him alive. That dread serpent, which is the terror of nearly every wild creature, is just another morsel for one of these roaming swine."

Wild boars often band together and do most of their feeding at night. They may either travel alone or in small herds and wander as far as twelve miles in a night. As they move they are quiet, nervous and always alert for any strange element in their environment.

It was Edward C. M. Richards who, after observing these animals in their native terrain in northern Germany, said, "They were astonishingly alert and active—as quick or even quicker on their feet than a collie dog in the pink of condition." Richards was amazed, as has been many a mountain man in the Smokies, at the speed with which these wild hogs can disappear in the woods by nimbly clearing ditches, downfall logs, and all manner of rough terrain. "The fact that they never stood still for more than a second or two," said Richards, "showed that they had the wild animal's appreciation for the fact that the price of liberty is constant vigilance."

When it is a sow's time to bear young, and this may come at any time of the year, she hides out among rocks, or in one of those thickets so dense the mountain people call them "laurel hells," and gives birth to a litter that usually numbers four or five pigs. When they are a year old the pigs are wearing permanent tusks. They reach sexual maturity half a year later.

The story of how the wild boar came to the Smokies is linked with the pattern of ownership in those hills prior to creation of the national forests and the Great Smoky Mountains National Park. According to popular misconception, the Smokies were owned by people who hunted squirrels, made whisky, feuded with each other, and assembled on rickety front porches to sing plaintive ballads. These mountain men, however, owned only patches of the Smokies. Vast holdings were in the names of great corporations interested mostly in the timber and usually based in some distant city or even a foreign country.

One such organization was the Great Smoky Mountain Land and Timber Company which on February 24, 1908, sold a vast acreage in the Smokies to the Whiting Manufacturing Company. The owners of this company, W. S. Whiting, and his brother Frank were Englishmen. At one time, when they needed a loan of $2,000,000, they engaged the services of George Gordon Moore, a professional adviser to English investors. Moore arranged the loan and helped close the deal.

So pleased were the Whitings that they rewarded Moore with what must have appeared to the financial world of the day as a strange type of reimbursement; they gave him permission to establish a game preserve on 1600 acres of timberland around Hooper Bald. Moore was thinking ahead, and he was thinking big. The shooting preserve, he felt, would be most useful as a place to entertain and influence wealthy investors.

Hooper Bald, which is a peak (elevation 5429 feet) in the

Snowbird Mountains of western North Carolina, was named for Dr. Enos Hooper, who helped explore the area. In the Great Smoky Mountains, a "bald" is a spot on the mountains which, for some complex climatic reasons, is void of trees in a land noted for its great trees. Hooper is one of many such balds.

By 1909 George Moore had hired local help and his unusual project was underway. The preserve was to include woodlands all around Hooper Bald. By Herculean effort they built a road up the mountainside to the top of the bald. In 1911 everything was in readiness to build enclosures to prevent the imported wild creatures from spreading out over the surrounding hills.

A mile of fence ten feet high was strung through the woods and nailed to trees. It enclosed 1500 acres. The new fence was spoken of in wonder up and down the hollows. Into the project went twenty-five tons of wire, all laboriously hauled up the mountain by oxen at the rate of a dollar per hundredweight. Along the top of the fence, workmen nailed three strands of barbed wire supported on arms which reached inward at a forty-five degree angle. Moore called this enclosure his "buffalo lot." The "boar lot," which covered 500 acres, was fenced with split rails nine rails high.

As April 1912 approached, excitement ran high in the little town of Murphy, North Carolina. Cargoes of strange foreign creatures were arriving on the railroad train. Among the animals were fourteen Russian wild hogs. Citizens around town had been expecting these wild hogs for several days and stories of their mean character and ferocity had spread up and down the hollows.

Waiting for the animals was a train of half a dozen ox teams hitched to wagons. The crates containing fourteen hogs and also four buffaloes were loaded on the wagons. With considerable urging the reluctant oxen put their shoulders to the yokes and started up the mountain. For three days they struggled to move their strange cargo over the twenty-five miles of trails. As the wagons arrived, the wild hogs were turned loose in the boar enclosure. Some of the neighbors had assembled to see the hogs turned out and, as one account tells it, ". . . as the beady-eyed tuskers whooshed from the crates, some of the mountaineers went shinnying up trees like scared squirrels. They had been used to wild mountain razorbacks and acorn-splitter hogs all their lives but these wild pigs from abroad were something different."

All through that summer, stock continued to arrive in Murphy and citizens there haven't seen anything like it before or since. Eventually the wagons had labored up the mountainside to Hooper's Bald carting with them a total of fourteen hogs, eight buffalo, fourteen elk, six mule deer from Colorado, and thirty-four bears, including nine Russian brown bears. Moore also had 200 wild turkeys and 10,000 ringneck pheasant eggs shipped in. The wild boar had their own pen, but everything else was turned out together in the big buffalo lot.

Then Moore purchased from local citizens 150 sheep and 150 turkeys to be delivered alive. These were turned out into the buffalo lot for the bears to feed on.

Meanwhile, George Moore had hired a local towheaded youngster named Garland "Cotton" McGuire to take charge of his game preserve. McGuire lived on Hooper's Bald for the next thirty-one years. Eventually he became a leading authority on the wild boar. But he never learned to love them. "They take the food that bears better deserve," he said. "They're just plain hateful animals."

Some of the animals, too, soon proved uncooperative. Among them were the bears that climbed the fence and came to the clubhouse for handouts. Several of them, it was learned, had grown up in zoos. Cotton McGuire soon found that it was no easy matter to get a bear back into the pen. The process has been described by Perry Jones. "In order to return a bear to the lot," says Jones, "two men would have to lasso each of his front feet, pull him around a tree, and securely bind both pairs of feet together on the opposite side of the tree. Next a pole was placed across the back of his neck, and his chin was pushed up firmly against the tree." In this manner the bear catchers could get a collar around the animal's neck and strap two chains to the collar. By holding the "extreme end" of each chain, they would keep the animal away from each other while they led him back to the enclosure.

Over the years the buffalo died one by one, and the bears disappeared. Poachers got the turkeys. It never was much trouble for the wild boars to get out of their split-rail enclosure and some made their escape early. Others come and went as the spirit moved them. But it was believed by Jones that most of them stayed inside and reproduced in the comparative freedom they found there because not for eight years following their arrival were they ever hunted.

Like a youngster with a new toy, George Moore gradually lost interest in his mountaintop game preserve. He hunted there only a few times although on several occasions he sent business acquaintances down to stay at the lodge and hunt.

Cotton McGuire's pay checks stopped coming sometime after Moore stopped visiting the project. The hard-pressed caretaker took legal action in an effort to get his money. Moore promptly wrote to McGuire and asked him to come to New York for a conference. In New York Moore handed McGuire a check for $1000, plus a document which was the title to the entire Hooper Bald game preserve. Moore had given him even the buildings and furniture. As Cotton McGuire made his way back to North Carolina he tried to figure out what in the world he could do with such a property. The hogs were easy enough; he knew what to do about them.

Back home he set a date for the first hunt those hills had ever known for European wild hogs. He invited his friends up the mountain and they came leading their packs of hounds. By this time the hogs had increased until there were between sixty and 100 inside the 500-acre pen. When the men and their dogs entered the boar pen for the big hunt, all hell broke loose. When the hunt was over, and it did not last long, only two hogs had been killed. Assorted hunters clung to precarious perches in the trees and a half-dozen of the finest hounds in the Snowbird Range lay dead or dying because they approached too closely to those ripping tusks. As for the hogs, the shooting and yelling had scarcely begun before they knocked the fence asunder and began escaping into the surrounding mountains. Their descendants roam there today.

McGuire sold the remaining elk and buffalo and, after the Whiting Manufacturing Company sold the property to a large paper company, went to work as a fire warden for the purchaser. Cotton McGuire died at the age of sixty-two on March 13, 1957. Today, if you climb to the top of Hooper's Bald, you can still find remnants of the old buildings and fences. It is now part of the Nantahala National Forest.

Each autumn hunters come to pursue the wild boar in the hills. It is likely that the pure-blooded European wild hogs have now been mixed with gone-wild razorbacks, but the end product is as mean and as wild as ever. And elusive. More often than not, the hunter is unsuccessful. The hunting of the wild hogs is controlled by the North Carolina Wildlife Resources Commission and the Tennessee Game and Fish Commission, who consider the wild hog an asset and not a liability in the Smokies. This is the oldest but not the only population of European wild hogs in America.

Across the country in California is another branch of this wild-hog family. The European wild boar came to California in 1924—from the mountain slopes around Hooper's Bald in North Carolina. McGuire had a request for the hogs, and, with the help of traps and dogs, he and a neighbor captured a dozen of the animals and shipped them to the West Coast.

The hogs, after their long trip across the country, were turned loose near Carmel on the San Francisquito Ranch not far from the Los Padres National Forest. Some of the hogs spread naturally into the forest and these were supplemented by a planting of two dozen yearlings into the forest's Carmel watershed in 1932.

Who had asked McGuire to send European wild hogs to the West Coast? The name is familiar; it was George Gordon Moore, who still admired the Russian hogs and wanted a stock of them for a new estate he was establishing in California.

One other area in the United States has a small population of wild European boars. In 1938 a hurricane swept across New Hampshire and made possible the escape of the European wild hogs held at Corbin's Park in Sullivan County. Their descendants are believed to number fewer than forty. And, in spite of the fact that they can be legally hunted the year round, their future seems as secure in their adopted New England stronghold as it is in California and in the Great Smoky Mountains where George Moore first introduced them.

SENTIMENT AND FOOL'S GOLD

Chapter 7

The Acclimatizers

———❦———

As he looked around the city of Cincinnati in 1872, Andrew Erkenbrecher was depressed by the fact that he no longer saw the wonderful little songbirds that had brightened the days of his youth back in Germany. Being a man of action, Erkenbrecher promptly embarked on a bold plan to correct this oversight. He would bring to Cincinnati the songbirds of Europe—and thus render this city on the banks of the Ohio a little more bearable for human beings.

Consequently, Erkenbrecher soon secured a large shipment of birds and arranged to move them out of the land where nature had kept them in balance with their environment. He would help them start life anew on the hills above the Ohio. And apparently he paused not for a moment to consider the immensity of the trouble this scheme might cause.

Erkenbrecher came from Germany at the age of fifteen and eventually amassed a considerable fortune. Among the hobbies he could then afford to indulge was the keeping of a multitude of pets, especially birds, in cages. This led to his founding the Cincinnati Zoological Garden, today one of the country's better-known institutions of its kind. Erkenbrecher possessed what was characterized by one writer of his day as ". . . a love for the beautiful."

He made no effort to hide his disappointment with the list of birds he found in this new country. After explaining how the European birds would aid people against the "encroachment of insects," Erkenbrecher promptly added, ". . . as well as enliven our parks, woods and meadows, which in comparison with European countries are so bare of feathered songsters."

While he was looking hopefully to European horizons for his twittering friends, knowledgeable ornithologists had already compiled impressive lists of birds native to Cincinnati. Half a century earlier, the restless John J. Audubon had worked in the city of Cincinnati and was impressed by the abundance of bird life in the Ohio Valley. There has been a list of more than 300 species of birds sighted in southwestern Ohio, and bird watchers taking the annual Christmas bird count have compiled a list of more than 120 species observed in the dead of winter.

Erkenbrecher announced that $5000 would be spent bringing European birds to Cincinnati. "It may be expected," he added, "that the ennobling influence of the song of birds will be felt by the inhabitants."

In and around Cincinnati the wood thrushes, orioles, yellow-breasted chats, warblers, and other birds of great variety sang on, as had their ancestors for countless centuries. These native songsters, among the finest in the world of birds, were blithely unaware that their musical talents were overlooked or unappreciated or that plans were afoot to have them share the stage with foreign intruders.

Erkenbrecher later reported to the Cincinnati Society of Natural History that his group had, during 1872–74, spent $9000 purchasing and importing European songbirds at an average price of about $4.50 a pair. They had brought in 4000 birds, including robin redbreast, wagtail, skylark, starling, dunnock, song thrush, blackbird, nightingale, goldfinch, siskin, great tit, dutch tit, dipper, Hungarian thrush, missel thrush, corn crake, and crossbill. It is also known that they imported house sparrows.

To acclimatize these imports to Cincinnati conditions, the Cincinnati Acclimatization Society housed them in the garret of a towering old mansion standing in a part of the city known as Burnet Woods. Then, on a morning in May, Erkenbrecher and some of his bird-loving associates released the immigrants from their lengthy captivity. If they aimed to influence these new birds with the beauty of the Ohio Valley, they could not have chosen their time more wisely. The month of May is the finest of the year through this valley. The meadows, lawns, and woodlands are green with tender new growth. The sun warms the land and flowers color the hillsides. Into such a world and on such a day the European "songsters" were introduced to their new terrain. What a morning to be released from an attic!

In the yard stood Andrew Erkenbrecher looking up at the attic window and directing the proceedings. Records reveal that "a few seconds more and a cloud of beautiful plumage burst through the open window, and a moment later Burnet Woods was resonate with a melody of thanksgiving never heard before and probably never heard since." (Almost certainly.)

Optimism ran high. But the unappreciative linnets soon vanished from Cincinnati and the nightingales went the way of the German bullfinches. For all the fine intentions of this and similar acclimatization societies across this land and others, failure greeted their efforts more often than success. Those who would shed a tear in sympathy should pause and consider those species for which the acclimatization societies can rightfully claim credit. Their outstanding success, if this is the word, is found in the stories of the house sparrows and the starlings which they helped spread around the world.

The acclimatization society working in Cincinnati had kindred spirits in widely scattered locations. "During the last fifty years," T. S. Palmer reported in the 1898 yearbook of the U. S. Department of Agriculture, "a number of acclimatization societies have been organized for the purpose of introducing animals and plants from foreign countries. Private individuals, too, have devoted both time and money to importing birds or mammals which they consider necessary or desirable additions to the native fauna. Four or five societies exist in New Zealand and several have been formed in the United States."

In New York, Eugene Scheifflin and John Avery were leaders in the American Acclimatization Society which would ultimately do such a "grand" job establishing the European starling.

In Oregon the Portland Song Bird Club, under the leadership of C. F. Pfluger, was one of the first to import English sparrows.

The Cincinnati Society of Natural History, in its bulletin in 1884, listed under "Zoological Miscellany" the birds introduced by Erkenbrecher. "While we deem the above facts of sufficient ornithological importance to merit a record in permanent form," said the editor stiffly, "and cannot but admire the sentiment which promoted the introduction of these birds, we may properly at some time express the opinion that the general principle is, zoologically speaking, a wrong one. . . ."

Chapter 8

Sparrows and Starlings

EARLY in 1886 Walter B. Barrows, a government ornithologist, embarked on a monumental fact-finding project designed to answer once and for all the inflammatory question of whether or not the imported house sparrow was good or bad for American agriculture. To many people it was a surprise that the question was still debated, or that the drab and unloved "English sparrow" had an apologist left in the land.

Barrows' plan was to gather all the evidence he could get on either side of the controversy. In his office in the United States Department of Agriculture in Washington he composed a questionnaire and mailed out 5000 copies seeking current opinion on the worth of this foreign bird in the New World.

In the weeks that followed, reports poured into Barrows' office. More than 3330 citizens took time to tell him their thoughts about house sparrows. A few said robins and Baltimore orioles were more destructive, but the verdict was overwhelming against the sparrows. "It strips down green corn in the fields," said one Massachusetts farmer, "sometimes one third or more the length of the ear, and is doing so now."

Another said, "I had a variety of wheat which I was growing for seed and they took every grain."

From New York a farmer wrote, "I know to my sorrow that it lives all winter entirely on grain, for in buying chicken feed, I allow two parts for the sparrows and one for the chickens."

"The sparrows," said an Ohio farmer bitterly, "are the worst birds we have." And his reaction summed up the feeling of the majority of farmers, a scant thirty-five years after the bird had made its first appearance in the United States.

If success for a transplanted wild creature is measured by its rate of reproduction and the speed with which it expands its territory, there could be no question that the house sparrow succeeded in this country. Biologically, those chattering, impudent house sparrows eating from your bird feeder and nesting in the eaves are among the most successful wild birds the world has ever seen. The house sparrow has more than doubled its territory within the past century, now occupies about a fourth of the earth's area and is still spreading.

Students of natural history believe that the house sparrow had its origin in the vicinity of the Mediterranean from which, many thousands of years ago, it spread eastward and northward, usually as an associate of man wherever new lands were cultivated.

In three decades, however, beginning about 1850, the house sparrow took over new territory faster than it ever had before or is likely to do again. During those years it immigrated to the United States, became established in South America, and was successfully introduced in Australia, Tasmania, New Zealand, and Hawaii. This was the age of the sparrow "craze." Homesick European immigrants around the world cherished memories of the sparrows known to them in their youth.

The sparrows were brought first to New York. The Brooklyn Institute appointed a committee to introduce house sparrows to the United States. Nicholas Pike, a member of the board of directors, was appointed chairman of the committee. Mr. Pike later recorded his own account of that project.

"It was not until 1850," he wrote, "that the first eight

pairs were brought from England to the Brooklyn Institute, of which I was then a director. We built a large cage for them and cared for them during the winter months. Early in the spring of 1851 they were liberated, but they did not thrive.

"In 1852 a committee of members of the Institute was chosen for the re-introduction of these birds, of which I was chairman.

"Over $200 was subscribed for expenses. I went to England in 1852, on my way to the consul-generalship of Portugal. On my arrival in Liverpool I gave the order for a large lot of Sparrows and song birds to be purchased at once. They were shipped on board the steam-ship *Europa*, if I am not mistaken, in charge of an officer of the ship. Fifty Sparrows were let loose at the Narrows, according to the instructions, and the rest on arrival were placed in the tower of Greenwood Cemetery chapel. They did not do well, so were removed to the house of Mr. John Hooper, one of the committee, who offered to take care of them during the winter.

"In the spring of 1853 they were let loose on the grounds of Greenwood Cemetery, and a man hired to watch them. They did well and multiplied, and I have original notes taken from time to time of their increase and colonization over our great country."

But the Brooklyn Institute and Nicholas Pike had no monopoly on this altruistic project. Bird lovers from many parts of the country were turning their eyes to Europe.

For a decade or more European bird dealers were confronted with eager Americans who came with faith, hope, and money, determined to purchase Europe's songbirds as their contribution to bringing beauty to the new world.

Sparrows were soon introduced to Portland, Maine, and to Peace Dale, Rhode Island. Some of the birds destined for Rhode Island, however, escaped in Boston when the ship docked and were never seen again. So a new planting of sparrows was carefully made in Boston Common a decade later. In 1860 a dozen of the imported sparrows—which had by now caught the fancy of bird lovers all over the country —were tenderly released in Madison Square. Four years later others were liberated in Central Park, where they would, in good time, be joined by the starlings. In the New York region a grand flock of 200 reserves were released in 1866 in Union Park.

Meanwhile, the sparrows were being released in such widely separated areas as Galveston, Texas, New Haven, Cleveland, Cincinnati, San Francisco, Salt Lake City, Halifax, Nova Scotia, and Quebec City. The largest recorded single release in this period of house-sparrow mania occurred in Philadelphia in the year 1869. The city government imported a thousand of the sparrows and turned them loose on the town.

"In many of the cases . . . ," wrote Barrows, "it is positively known that the Sparrows were brought to this country from the Old World, and mainly, if not entirely, from Great Britain and Germany. But no sooner had they become fairly numerous at any of these points than people began to take them hence to other places, sometimes in large numbers, but more often only a few pairs at a time. In most cases these few birds were carefully watched, protected and fed."

The ornithologist Arthur Cleveland Bent left a clear description of the tender care lavished on these hardy birds. In his famed series of life histories of North American birds published by the Smithsonian Institution, Bent wrote, "Many years ago, when I was a small boy, probably in the late 1860's or early 1870's my uncle, who lived next door to us in Taunton, Massachusetts, was the first to introduce English sparrows into that immediate vicinity. He built a large flying cage in his garden that was roofed over, covered with netting on four sides, and well supplied with perches and nesting boxes. Here the sparrows were so well fed and cared for that they soon began to breed. It was not long before the cage became overcrowded, and he ordered his coachman to put up numerous nesting boxes all over the place and to liberate the sparrows. They soon filled all the new boxes, and also drove away the purple martins, tree swallows, and house wrens from all the old boxes. When the neighbors' cats killed a few of the pugnacious sparrows, which were the newest pets and were zealously guarded, my uncle became so angered that he ordered his coachman to 'kill every cat in the neighborhood.' My uncle drove in that night to find the coachman with nine of the neighbors' cats laid out on the stable floor."

From Strathroy, Ontario, Barrows had received a letter from Mr. L. H. Smith, who was credited with introducing sparrows to his home community. "In March, 1874," Smith wrote, "I sent to a New York bird dealer, and he forwarded me per express, twelve birds, six males and six females, at a cost to me of $1 each. If all the sparrows in our town are mine, and my neighbors all say they are, then I have at least plenty for my money. . . . They are now [October 11, 1886] in thousands in our town, and are plentiful in every town, city, and village in this part of Ontario. . . ."

America was the sparrows' promised land. The living was good. The birds industriously carried nesting materials from stable and hen yard and draped straw, feathers, and string beneath the eaves of man's buildings. For food they had only to clean up around the grain elevators, glean from the fields, and follow horses in the village streets.

The sparrows were brought into some communities expressly to control the caterpillars. Apparently those responsible were unaware of the fact that the hair on many of the caterpillars would have proved injurious to sparrows if they had eaten them. Instead of eating the caterpillars, the sparrows probably harassed some of four native bird species known to prey on these insects—the robin, Baltimore oriole, yellow-billed cuckoo, and black-billed cuckoo. Consequently, the caterpillars may have benefited by the coming of the house sparrow.

They were soon widely despised for the injury they did to decorative plants around homes and public buildings. They roosted in the vines and trees and in some cases killed the vegetation with their excrement. They destroyed some of the English ivy on the outside of the Smithsonian Institution in Washington, D.C. During a two-month period in 1884 the sexton of St. John's Church in Providence, Rhode Island, removed from the vines around the church two cartloads of nesting materials and destroyed 970 sparrow eggs.

The sparrow was known to destroy the buds and blossoms of fruit trees in spring and later damage the ripening fruit. Grain crops are favorites of these seed eaters, and it was soon noticed that they made great inroads on the wheat crop. As the grain began to ripen, the old birds and their new young of the year congregated and moved into the country-side in what one farmer called ". . . foraging parties for excursions into the country."

It was inevitable that time, events, and the habits of the sparrow would alter the sentiment the populace once held for this bold little bird which had taken so readily to life in the streets. Barrows and his fellow scientists had begun to realize, by this year of 1889, the seriousness of the sparrow situation. ". . . it is only within the past year," he wrote, "that we have come to realize something of the magnitude of the 'craze' which led so many people to foster and distribute this serious pest. It is impossible to mark the precise date," he added, "at which the tide of public opinion turned against the sparrow."

It was a gradual realization, a tardy and reluctant awakening.

Bent's uncle, who so carefully fostered the sparrows and protected them from all outside forces, was soon to change his mind. "It was not long, however," wrote Bent, "before my uncle began to miss the martins, swallows, and wrens and to realize that the sparrows were not as desirable as he expected: so he ordered the coachman to reduce them. This he did effectively by digging a trench and filling it with grain, so that he could kill large numbers with a single raking shot. But the martins, swallows, and wrens never returned."

The reaction of people to sparrows was tied closely to the abundance of the birds in the neighborhood. It was easy enough to get along with a few house sparrows, but, as they began to overrun the towns, the birds' former benefactors began taking down the sparrow houses and discontinuing the spreading of grain for them.

In West Chester, Pennsylvania, in 1879, Dr. B. H. Warren, speaking before the Microscopical Society, issued this plea: "We ask all lovers of birds—and who among us do not admire, nay love, the native songsters—to lend their aid, and speedily too, that some means may be devised for the blotting out of this unlooked-for bane."

Towns were now revoking regulations passed to protect the sparrows. Pennsylvania, whose largest city had released 1000 English sparrows, now passed a new law in 1883 stating that: ". . . from and after the passage of this act it shall be lawful at any season of the year to kill or in any way destroy the small bird known as the English Sparrow."

Michigan, beginning on March 15, 1887, offered a penny each for dead sparrows in lots of twenty-five or more. Such futile efforts against the sparrow became common in communities frustrated by the bird's population explosion.

The unfathomable thing in all this is that these bad habits of the house sparrow were well known to farmers in Great Britain long before the birds were caught up and brought to the United States. There had been Sparrow Clubs in England long before the sparrow "craze" hit this country. Nearly every parish had one or more of these neighborhood organizations which paid for destruction of house sparrows and their eggs because the birds were a threat to crops. Such clubs existed as early as 1744.

Practical English farmers must have scratched their heads in disbelief at the reports of American buyers coming all the way across the Atlantic to place their orders for house sparrows. Fruit grower Jabez Webster of Centralia, Illinois, after extensive travels in Europe, reported in 1886 that one astonished farmer in the county of Norfolk told him that in England, ". . . they had been spending money to destroy sparrows for fifty years and still had to spend money."

Meanwhile, W. T. Hill, an enterprising Indianapolis citizen, began trapping sparrows to replace the pigeons used in live pigeon shoots at gun clubs around the country. A house sparrow makes a difficult mark for a shotgunner. Hill reported in 1887 that about seventy-five per cent of the birds he shipped for this purpose were killed by the shooters. The twenty-five per cent that got away, he believed, were a "drop in the bucket." He discounted the possibility that he was in any manner aiding the spread of the English sparrow. He figured that he caught and shipped a total of 40,000 sparrows. If one fourth escaped the guns, Hill alone might have sent 10,000 sparrows to new homes throughout the Midwest. Ultimately, of course, they would have reached these neighborhoods anyhow, and in all fairness to the enterprising Hill, many of the communities to which he shipped birds already had them established.

Some people, recalling that sparrows were considered edible in parts of Europe, began looking at the birds hungrily. Shortly they were being offered on restaurant and boarding-house menus, often as "reed birds." In 1887 house sparrows were bringing a dollar a hundred on the Albany, New York, market. Or, if you just wanted to make a family-sized pot pie, you could buy a dozen for twenty-five cents. On November 18, 1887, the Albany *Express* reported: "One game and poultry dealer in town has thus far bought and then sold to others about three thousand, eight hundred of the little pests. They make excellent pot-pie and are regarded as excellent eating by those who have made the trial. The flavor is said to be somewhat like that of reed birds and much superior to that of quail."

On New York's Third Avenue a boardinghouse propri-
etress was capturing dozens of sparrows by spreading oats
in her back yard. Once caught, the sparrows were fattened
a few days on oats, then prepared with a little wooden
skewer, a bit of bacon draped across them, and basted until
brown—following which they were declared a "great deli-
cacy" by her boarders. The New York *Times*, remarking on
this development, predicted that as soon as this knowledge
spread ". . . no boardinghouse meal would be deemed in
good form unless a dish of fat sparrows adorns it."

The bird has now spread through the United States and
southward throughout Mexico. Spanish monks brought them
to Havana in 1850 and today there are house sparrows
throughout Cuba. The first South American release was in
1872 when twenty pairs were turned out in Buenos Aires in
the vain hope that they would control harmful moths. The
sparrow was later introduced to other parts of the continent, including Brazil in 1903, here again with the hope of
bringing an insect under control. The sparrows engaged in a
great population explosion in South America. They now
blanket the southern half of the continent.

Nor are the sparrows done yet. Scientists anticipate that
they will move into still larger areas of the earth's surface
not yet invaded, including China, additional parts of Siberia
and South America, and probably western Australia in spite
of efforts to stop them.

People in most parts of the world have belatedly recognized the house sparrow for his true nature. Consequently,
he is seldom taken on free rides any longer to new territories.
Among birds, his is a tale of outstanding success. But he
owes to man a genuine debt of gratitude. So does the starling,
which in recent times has become a pest of even greater
proportions than the house sparrow.

It is easy for people to hate starlings. We dislike their
aggressive behavior toward birds of milder manner, their

gluttonous consumption of farm and garden products intended for human nourishment, their habit of congregating in massive, noisy flocks to feed or roost; and even their swaggering walk. But, most of all, people despise starlings for their unbounded fecundity, because starlings do nothing in moderation.

Were it not, in fact, for the starling's magnificent ability to populate the earth beyond the point which people consider reasonable, this aggressive black bird might get along moderately well with his human neighbors. At least there would be less of a reason for starling haters to curse the memory of Eugene Scheifflin.

Nature granted the starling a breeding territory reaching from Norway to Siberia and south to the Mediterranean. In autumn these birds frequently migrate to North Africa and India or spend the winter in the relatively warm climates of Spain or other Mediterranean countries.

Given the advantage of hindsight, it is easy to say that men would have been wise to let it go at that. During the last part of the nineteenth century, however, bird lovers transplanted these aggressive birds to several new parts of the world, usually in the belief that the starling's insect-eating habits would make it a major economic asset.

It should be noted here that in 1890, the year the starling was first successfully introduced to the United States, it had already been established for two decades in New Zealand, where it had quickly built up large populations that damaged agricultural crops. "Much has been said concerning the advantages of introducing the starling into this country," wrote T. S. Palmer, biologist with the U. S. Biological Survey in 1898, "but in spite of the many arguments brought forward, the bird's character is not above suspicion, and its usefulness is still open to question. The fact seems to have been overlooked that in other countries the starling has signally failed to fulfill the expectations concerning its usefulness. Certainly the experience of Australia and New Zealand offers little encouragement. It was introduced in New Zealand in 1867, and as early as 1870 was reported as 'becoming very numerous.' It seems to have increased very rapidly, and in spite of its natural preference for insects, in its new home it has adopted a fruit diet to such an extent as to become a great pest. In South Australia it was reported to be common in certain localities in 1894, and measures for its extermination were considered."

The fact that the bird had begun to display these unwelcome characteristics in other parts of the world where it had been introduced was no deterrent to the starling's American admirers. Trial introductions were hopefully, but unsuccessfully carried out in Massachusetts and New Jersey in 1844, Portland, Oregon, in 1889 and 1892, and Pennsylvania and Massachusetts in 1897. Some were released at Bay Ridge, New York, about 1900, two years after Palmer's warnings appeared in the official U. S. Department of Agriculture yearbook. One after the other, these early efforts failed. The man who proved equal to the challenge of establishing the starling in this country, however, was Eugene Scheifflin, a New York drug manufacturer whose hobbies were the study of birds and the study of Shakespeare. He was the leading force in the American Acclimatization Society in New York. Being interested in both birds and Shakespeare as he was, he might be expected to notice the birds mentioned in Shakespeare's writings. It was even natural enough, perhaps, that he should make a list of them. But who would have guessed that his next project would be to import to America all the birds Shakespeare had mentioned? As unusual as this method for selecting foreign wildlife for introduction may seem, one must admit that there is about as much logic and study behind it as there was behind the other selections Americans were making from Europe's bird list during that period. And even if *Henry IV* had never contained the line, "Nay, I'll have a starling shall be taught to speak nothing but 'Mortimer,'" in all probability we would have brought starlings here sooner or later.

The same year Scheifflin's starlings were introduced they began nesting. The first of their nests was found across from Central Park beneath the eaves of the northeast wing of The American Museum of Natural History, perhaps the birthplace of the first wild starlings ever hatched in the United States.

During the following years ornithologists observed that as starling populations built up in an area, the birds engaged in fall and winter excursions into new territories. Within five years following such exploration they established breeding populations. Then, as population pressures in the new areas grew, the fall and winter wanderings sent more starlings on to seek still other territories. In this manner, starlings spread out from their point of origin in Central Park and began their transcontinental advance.

Within six years the starlings had spread around Long Island, Brooklyn, and near-by suburbs. In fact, there were already a few people viewing starlings as dirty, noisy neighbors.

By 1915 starlings were established residents of Halifax, Nova Scotia. Two years later one was found at Savannah, Georgia, and in another decade they were being seen frequently in Wisconsin, Illinois, Iowa, and south into Mississippi and Louisiana. Meanwhile, back in New York, they had become the most abundant of all birds.

By 1916 the U. S. Bureau of Biological Survey had already begun an extensive research program designed to ". . . ascertain the economic status of the starling in the United States." The big question in the minds of many rural people was whether or not the starling was destined to become as much of a pest as the house sparrow. By 1928 the starling range was usually spoken of as anywhere east of the Mississippi River.

When a circular discussing the spread of the starling came

out of the Department of Agriculture in 1928, ornithologists were still wondering how far west the bird would expand. "The area of the Great Plains, with its scarcity of suitable nesting sites," said the Department of Agriculture, "will undoubtedly retard the westward advance; whether or not it will prove a complete barrier cannot now be foreseen. If the Plains are passed, the Rocky Mountains will present another barrier, but if both are passed the species may be expected to extend its range to the Pacific."

Any dim hopes that the Great Plains and the Rocky Mountains might hold back the surging starling population were soon laid to rest.

Starlings had been unsuccessfully introduced at Portland, Oregon, in 1889 and 1892; the West Coast had to wait until the birds could spread out naturally from the East. "The introduction from which North America's population actually derives (probably entirely)," says M. T. Myres, of the University of British Columbia's Department of Zoology, "was that of 1890 and 1891 in New York. From this locus the bird has been moving steadily west until it has reached the country west of the Continental Divide." From New York, where Scheifflin turned them free, it had taken the starlings fifty-five years to spread to British Columbia. "The Rocky Mountain chain," says Myres, "seems to have been no barrier at all to the passage of the species westward." On April 17, 1952, a starling was observed near Juneau, Alaska. It is now present in all of the fifty states.

The wintering flocks of starlings began mingling with other blackbirds, often in enormous flocks. In 1961 a government biologist with the U. S. Fish and Wildlife Service computed that there were 4,500,000 blackbirds nesting within a fifty-mile radius of Washington, D.C. It was generally believed that they were still increasing and no one knew how fast. There were numerous roosts where several millions of them assembled on winter nights. The biggest of all the known blackbird roosts was in Virginia's famed Dismal

Swamp, where an estimated 20,000,000 blackbirds funneled in at the end of each day, a large percentage of them starlings.

Blackbirds congregating in such masses have become serious plagues. They cause damage in four main classifications. Through the beef-feeding lots of the Midwest and western states, starlings flock to consume grain spread for cattle. Feed which they do not steal directly they often contaminate and ruin.

Livestock specialists place the blackbird damage in western feed lots in the millions of dollars each year. Starlings are considered the chief offenders in twelve western states and five Corn Belt states. Farmers, especially through the Midwest, are also concerned by the fact that these birds, flying from one hog lot to the other, can carry swine diseases. The starlings eat corn, grain sorghums, rice, truck crops, and fruits and will eat one to two times their own body weight daily. This totals up to staggering quantities donated by American agriculture to descendants of Eugene Scheifflin's imported starlings.

In the Willamette Valley in Oregon, where holly is a high value commercial crop, roosting starlings so contaminate the leaves that the crops are ruined for market. One witness before a congressional committee studying blackbird depredations reported that, during 1958–59, starling damage to this crop sometimes ran as high as $1500 an acre in a single winter.

Residents of large cities know the starling as a pest that roosts on ledges above the sidewalks and flocks to city parks and playfields. Cities have found varied strange methods of combating these avian troublemakers. In some cities crews of police and local volunteers perch on the roofs of downtown buildings and blast at the starlings with shotguns. This helps momentarily. Some try electrical wires along the window ledges. Others display stuffed owls and a variety of noise makers designed to disturb the birds. Unfortunately, to be heard by birds, such sounds must be kept within the range audible to the human ear.

Strings of firecrackers are hung in orchards, and automatic exploders boom periodically in cornfields. Research specialists at Pennsylvania State College developed a technique for playing starling distress calls to frighten the birds. They caught some starlings and recorded their frantic calls as they were held in the hand. Such recordings have occasionally been successful.

When word of this experiment reached the Federal Aviation Agency in Washington, there was high interest, because the most dramatic of all the starlings' acts of vandalism is their threat to aircraft.

In October 1960 a Lockheed Electra jet departing from Boston's Logan International Airport was only twenty-five seconds off the ground when a flock of 10,000 or more starlings flew into its path. The big plane shuddered, stalled, and crashed. Sixty-two people were killed. After investigation at the Indianapolis laboratories of the Civil Aeronautics Board, officials concluded that starlings had been swept into the plane's two-foot wide air scoops and caused the number one, two, and four engines to flame out. This was a dramatic but not a unique case. Consequently, the Federal Aviation Agency became one of several agencies concerned about methods of controlling nuisance birds; something more lasting than the crews of starling chasers which some airports had put to work scaring birds off the runways.

Starlings captured by the Fish and Wildlife Service were taken to the Civil Aeronautics Administration sound room where the birds' distress calls were recorded by a microphone. The tapes were played from the fourth-story window of the Archives Building as flocks of starlings approached the building for the night. Thereafter the starlings no longer roosted on that side of the "treated" building in spite of the fact that they continued to roost on the back of the same building.

Biologists with the Fish and Wildlife Service, however, were looking for more permanent ways to reduce the starling damage. Huge floodlights set up near the roosts attracted the starlings into great funnel-shaped wire cages. But whatever dents the biologists could make destroying starlings with their mechanical methods, the starlings could quickly repair with their biotic potential.

Currently the federal government maintains two research centers where such problem birds as starlings, cowbirds and red-winged blackbirds are studied. In these research centers at Patuxent, Maryland, and Denver, Colorado, highly skilled biologists still search for the elusive answers on how to cope with the starling problem, and one of their major dreams is that they will discover some substance or method with which they can reduce the starling's efficiency in reproducing its kind.

Chapter 9

How the Gray Squirrels Invaded England

————— ✣ —————

THE English citizen, with his everlasting affection for small wild creatures, was certain sometime to become attracted to the American gray squirrel. By now the English have learned the hard way that they might better have resisted their urge to transport gray squirrels from the woodlands of eastern North America to the forests of the British Isles, where, instead of restricting their diet to nuts and other common squirrel food, they turned to eating the bark from valuable trees.

One can understand the appeal of this alert tree-climbing rodent. In his native North America this squirrel is warmly regarded by the populace. Game laws give him some protection most of the year. Hunters have long known the gray squirrel as a genuine challenge to the woodsman's stealth and hunting skills. Meanwhile, the gray squirrel has moved to town to dwell in public parks. Here he leaps nimbly from limb to limb to the amusement of all who see him. And the squirrel seems well adjusted to life in town.

Recently in downtown Columbus, Ohio, government planners advanced the progressive thought that there should be a great and costly new parking lot beneath the state capitol building. Was there a furor raised over the growing tax burden? Was anything said about the trees and the grass that would be disturbed? No. The matter of genuine public concern centered on the fate of a few dozen gray squirrels living in the trees around the building. The squirrels on the statehouse lawn had long been an attraction. Legislators scurrying from hotel to committee room paused to feed them peanuts. Children chased them gleefully and contented old men sat happily in the sun watching the show.

The governor, being an astute politician, realized that the gray squirrels merited his personal protection. Before any construction could begin, crews of expert wildlife specialists advanced on the capitol grounds. They caught as many of the squirrels as they could entice into their live traps and whisked them from town in good health to be released in farm woodlots near by.

Chances are good that the transplanted squirrels, denied their peanut handouts, faced a winter reminiscent of that encountered by the Pilgrim fathers on these shores, and the predators likely made fast work of many of them. But the public had been satisfied that a benevolent government had done all in its power to preserve the beloved squirrels from man's advancing concrete jungle.

There was a time in the history of North America when the gray squirrel seemed in genuine trouble in areas of excessive timbering. His numbers were dwindling rapidly in the late years of the nineteenth century. It is believed that some of those who first decided to transplant populations of gray squirrels to England might have considered this an important step in saving them from possible extinction. Others wanted them for pets.

With typical thoroughness, the British scientists have studied the advance of the imported gray squirrels across their islands. According to zoologist Monica Shorten, who did lengthy and meticulous research on the gray squirrel problem for Oxford University's Bureau of Animal Population, the most important lot of gray squirrels in English history was a shipment of ten that arrived in 1890. The animals were taken abroad by G. S. Page from New Jersey. Page presented them to the Duke of Bedford, who gratefully released them on his estate at Woburn.

Gray squirrels prospered so well there that the duke's estate later supplied squirrels for at least eight plantings in other parts of England. During the next two decades, still more animals were brought in from North America to bolster the expanding squirrel populations in the British Isles. Many were kept as caged pets, but they frequently chewed their way out of their cages and escaped to the woodlands.

Even after the importations of gray squirrels ceased, perhaps about 1910, they were still caught and transplanted to new territories around the islands. Today the gray squirrel, which has not yet completed his advance across England, Scotland, and Ireland, has fallen into disfavor among those who once welcomed him ashore.

But there was little that could be done to stem the advance of the agile rodents. Bounties were tried and free cartridges were offered to hunters, but with little effect. Meanwhile, English ecologists divided a map of the country into ten-kilometer square grids, each of which bounded sixty-four square miles.

In 1930 the foreign squirrels were found to occupy grids representing 9920 square miles. Five years later the figure had nearly doubled to 18,688 square miles, and by 1937 they occupied 21,120 square miles. That, incidentally, was the year the British government passed a regulation prohibiting the importation of gray squirrels and made it an offense against the Crown to keep them as pets. In 1959 the "gray squirrel explosion," as the British now called it, was still advancing. That year, according to studies by H. G. Lloyd, gray squirrels were found in 1072 of the 1638 grid squares in England and Wales. Now the advance seemed less dramatic, but the ecologists felt that the squirrels were spreading to occupy new territories within the grids where they had already been recorded, thus securing their conquests. "If the rate of spread shown over the past ten years were to be maintained," said Monica Shorten in the December 1964 issue of NATURAL HISTORY, "the squirrel might celebrate the centenary of its arrival by colonizing the entire land surface of England and Wales."

In fairness, it should be pointed out that the grid system may exaggerate the gray squirrel population. There may be, and often are, wide areas within the occupied grids where no gray squirrels are found.

One question that concerned English wildlife specialists during the advance of the American gray squirrel was the effect the intruder might have on the gentler little red squirrel, the only native tree squirrel in the British Isles. The English red squirrel is smaller than the gray squirrel and lacks the scrappy temper of red squirrels found in North America. The English red squirrels have declined and disappeared from many parts of England as the grays established themselves. One suggested reason was that the gray squirrels might have imported diseases to which the native squirrels had no immunity. No one knows whether or not this is true. Nor can they yet be certain whether or not the decline in native squirrels is due to competition for food, or perhaps to stress exerted by simply having to share the woodlands with the larger gray American.

But there can be no question that the red squirrel population has declined. The grid square studies revealed this. In 1945 the figures showed red squirrels gone from sixty-six per cent of those squares they formerly occupied and where gray squirrels had been established for fifteen years or more. The longer the gray squirrels live in an area the less likely there are to be red squirrels there. In one fourteen-year period gray squirrels advanced from 708 squares to 1072. Meanwhile, the areas occupied by red squirrels had dropped from 1011 to 571.

In England, however, the gray squirrel is most disliked for its relentless destruction of valuable hardwood trees. Hardly had the animal invaded the islands than he displayed a taste for the bark of trees instead of the nuts he was supposed to favor. As the squirrel numbers increased, so did the damage to woodlands. Why he began barking trees once in the British Isles is a matter of speculation. We do know that the damage occurs from April to July when normal food supplies are low. The gray squirrels restrict their bark stripping to broad-leafed trees and, although they have been known to damage a dozen or more species, most of the damage is to young beeches and maples, in valuable cultivated woodlands where timber is a managed crop. They completely girdle and kill many trees and kill or disfigure parts of others.

Scientists have made the fascinating suggestion that some strains of squirrels are more likely to be bark strippers than are their cousins. If all the gray squirrels in England ate bark between April and July, the damage, according to Monica Shorten, would be far worse than it is.

It has even been suggested by English scientists that the gray squirrels trapped and transplanted across the Atlantic were not our normal nut-loving gray squirrels, but really individuals trapped as nuisances in the United States and deported because they ate bark from trees. Once free on the English countryside, this speculation continues, the outlaw squirrels inbred and thus intensified their genetic tendencies to eat bark. This questionable line of reasoning gives some early squirrel trappers credit for being more diabolical than they were. Americans could hardly have been that angry about the English sparrow and the starling.

Chapter 10

New Frontiers for the Muskrats

AT first glance the muskrat is an unimpressive, plain-looking wetland rodent whose modest size would hardly attract attention. Through the early history of frontier exploration in North America, this two- to four-pound creature stood in the shadow of the beaver, fox, and mink. But the muskrat eventually came through as the most valuable furbearer in the country.

Native to most of North America, the muskrat was found here in the marshes, ponds, and sluggish rivers where it survived primarily on aquatic vegetation. It made its home, as it does today, either in burrows dug along the edges of waterways or "houses" built of marsh vegetation to protrude above the water's surface. Here the female usually bears three litters of young muskrats (known by trappers in some areas as "mice") per year and averages six to eight young per litter.

With this biotic potential working in their favor, muskrats annually grow vast quantities of fur. North American trappers harvest some 15,000,000 muskrats every year. Some years ago a Wisconsin mammalogist, Hartley H. T. Jackson, estimated the annual value of trapped muskrats in this country to be $12,000,000 by figuring pelt prices at a conservative eighty cents each.

Then if you compute the added effect on the economy from processing, manufacturing, and selling muskrat furs you begin to get a picture of the impact of this inconspicuous little aquatic creature upon the human economy. Jackson placed the worth of the muskrat at a figure not less than $100,000,000 a year. What is more, the muskrat prospers in habitats where it seldom competes with agricultural crops.

With its fur value, the muskrat was certain to attract attention in other parts of the world. One can understand why Europeans might reach out eagerly at the opportunity of transplanting muskrats to their own wetlands. Once established in Russia's vast marshlands, the animal became a valued addition to the fur resources there. In other parts of Europe, however, the story was not quite this uncomplicated.

The muskrat's first successful invasion of Europe occurred near Prague, Czechoslovakia, in 1905, when Prince Colleredo-Mannsfeld released two males and three females shipped in from Alaska. He is believed to have reinforced this little invasion force with a later shipment from Canada. From these initial introductions muskrats spread, as one biologist described it, ". . . like ripples from a pebble thrown into a pond. . . ."

The muskrat, once he has established his home territory, does not wander far afield. But the young ones, with no territories of their own yet established, can and often do travel considerable distances, often overland, to new territories. Those released in Czechoslovakia radiated from the original point of introduction and are said to have extended their range in the next several years by thirty to forty-five miles annually. From Czechoslovakia they invaded eastern Germany, Rumania, Yugoslavia, Poland, and eastern Russia.

In 1927 or 1928 the muskrats were invited into France. It was believed that they would be highly successful animals when raised in captivity for their fur. The French fur farmers soon learned, however, that muskrats do not prosper when crowded. If population pressures get too severe, their productivity falls. "To satisfy the biological requirements of this

1. *The Barbary sheep is a new resident of New Mexico. Pictured below, in the Canadian River Canyon of northeastern New Mexico, is a Barbary sheep ewe with its lamb. Photographs by the New Mexico Department of Game and Fish.*

2. *A familiar sight in picture books about African wildlife, but the setting is New Mexico. Photographs by the New Mexico Department of Game and Fish.*

3. *A matter of pride for the animal movers, the ringneck pheasant and his first successful American sponsor, Judge Owen N. Denny, and his wife. Photographs by the Oregon Game Commission and the Oregon Historical Society.*

4. *Another source of pride, the brown trout. Photograph by Edwin A. Bauer.*

5. *The Russian boar of Tennessee. Photograph by David Murrian, courtesy of the Tennessee Game and Fish Commission.*

6. *Two highly successful immigrants, the English sparrow and the starling. Photographs by Karl H. Maslowski.*

7. *The mongoose was brought to Jamaica to kill rats. Photograph by John H. Gerard.*

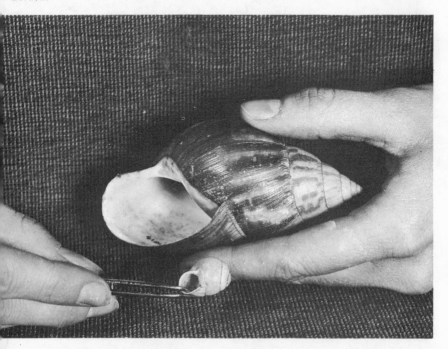

8. *The Giant African Land Snail, an unlikely star in a comedy of errors. Photograph courtesy of The American Museum of Natural History.*

9. *The Canada goose, a trophy bird in North America, became a pest when released in New Zealand. Photograph by the author.*

ungovernable rodent," said French biologist E. Bourdelle in 1939, "it was necessary to give it semi-freedom."

Given semi-freedom these aquatic escape artists were soon loose on the countryside and spreading out from the points of release much the same as they had done earlier in the century in Czechoslovakia. The first wild ones were caught in France in 1930. By 1933 officials figured that they had a full dozen centers of infestation—which is the term they were now using. Five of these trouble spots were in the agriculturally rich basins of the Seine and the Somme. From then on the American muskrat spread across Europe in what biologists characterized as the outstanding instance of successful acclimatization among mammals in the present century.

Those that had their start in Czechoslovakia eventually reached the German border and promptly invaded. They were first reported in Austria and Poland in the winter of 1929–30. Two years later the Polish government passed a law making anyone who transported muskrats liable to six months in prison and a fine of 2000 zloty.

Soon all those Europeans who considered themselves muskrat fanciers had reason to reconsider the scaly-tailed little aquatic rodents they had imported. The muskrats demonstrated their skill at tunneling by burrowing into dikes and banks of drainage ditches. This let a lot of water escape. They also tunneled into railroad and bridge embankments, creating a serious hazard to men and machinery. The muskrats also became pests when they started feeding on agricultural crops.

The first major effort to bring them under control was in 1917 in Bavaria. The infestations had passed the point where there was hope of exterminating the muskrat, so the German officials decided to halt the animal's westward advance. The government established a line of defense, called it the "Sperline," and from Munich to Regensburg trappers on the Sperline were ordered to deal death to all the muskrats they could find. That year the German government paid the muskrat trappers $8668. Officials felt this should have been enough to halt the advancing muskrats. But it wasn't. A few still slipped through the defenses. Then came the world-wide depression and there was no longer as much money to pay out for muskrat trapping.

Meanwhile, the first muskrats freed in the British Isles were apparently a few turned loose in Scotland in 1927. That year others were released in County Tipperary in Ireland and at Shoeburyness, Essex.

On March 17, 1932, England passed its destructive imported animals act, making it illegal to keep muskrats without a license. A year later the English government passed a new law. Now it was absolutely *forbidden* either to transport the animals or keep them alive. England by now had its crews of muskrat trappers scurrying about the countryside in lorries loaded with boats and other equipment suited to their mission. About this time the government sent to Bavaria, where the muskrat problem was an older one, and borrowed perhaps the most successful muskrat trapper in all of Bavaria. This master trapper, Herr Roith, journeyed to England where he demonstrated for the British crews his own methods of fighting muskrats. He carried a long metal probe which he pushed through the roof of muskrat tunnels. This chased muskrats out the entrance of their home to tumble into a trap the tricky Bavarian had set there for them. The British campaign against the muskrat lasted from 1932 to 1937, during which time it accounted for the demise of 2989 muskrats—at a cost of $28.29 each.

In Scotland, not only did they catch muskrats in their traps but also at least 6587 other unfortunate creatures, including 1745 Norway rats, 2305 water voles, fifty-seven weasels, thirty-six stoats, 2178 moorhens, 113 ducks, twenty-three gulls, thirteen blackbirds, and one eel.

Unlike other European countries, England was finally able to exterminate her muskrats.

In 1934, however, with the muskrats on the continent still

advancing, there were 137 licensed government trappers working on the problem in Saxony. They wore special armbands and their pay was the skin of the muskrat plus thirty to fifty pfennigs each, depending on how abundant the muskrats were in their assigned territory. Officials, however, had serious doubts concerning the infallibility of this plan. They worried, perhaps with justification, about the reported practice of trappers' always leaving a little nucleus of breeding stock behind—a type of biological social security. Muskrats were now established in most of Belgium, and trappers in Holland were working to keep the animals in check.

In Finland, however, the muskrat became a valued fur resource, as it did in Russia. In Japan, where muskrats were originally introduced from America, they are apparently restricted to an area around Tokyo.

For the most part, Europeans came to recognize the importation of the muskrat as a mistake and to wish they had left it swimming around in the marshes of North America. In Europe, profits from fur and meat failed to approach the great losses from repairs to dikes, dams, canals, highways, and bridges, and the losses of crops.

Chapter 11

Stranger from Argentina

___❧___

On a dark blustery December morning in 1946, a northern
Ohio farmer went into his hog house to feed the pigs, completely unprepared for what he found there. Eating with the
pigs was a strange animal. It could not be a beaver because,
instead of being flat, the animal's tail was more like that of
a rat. And it could not be a muskrat because this animal was
six times as large as a muskrat.

Very quietly the farmer backed out of the hog house, and
very quickly he went to the house to fetch the 12-gauge.
One shot did it. He could now examine the creature closely.
But this did not help, because he had never before seen anything like it. Later in the day the game protector came out,
and together they weighed and measured the invader. Then
they shipped it off to Columbus where biologists with the
state's Division of Wildlife took one look and pronounced
the creature a nutria, or coypu.

The nutria had no business in a hog house in northern
Ohio. His native habitat, in fact, was South America. Colonies of these creatures, however, had been established in
several parts of this country, especially to the south in the
marshes of coastal Louisiana and Texas. By the 1940s there
were colonies of these foreign furbearers established with
varying degrees of success in California, the Pacific Northwest, Colorado, New Mexico, and several additional states.
Most of them were first introduced as captives by people

convinced they were about to reap the greatest fortune in furs since Vitus Bering discovered the sea otter. In the years following, the bitter fur farmers were to discover the full extent to which this creature had failed them, and by then it would be too late to call back all the descendants of "gone wild" nutria.

Although the nutria bears superficial resemblances to both the beaver and the muskrat, neither could claim him as a close relative. The average muskrat weighs about three pounds, but the nutria established in wild Louisiana populations weighs seventeen pounds. The nutria, or coypu as it is known in its native South America, measures twenty-four inches long and has a round scaled tail that adds sixteen inches to its length. Its short round ears can be closed tight when it submerges. It has a short flat head, long curved yellow teeth, and beady little eyes.

The fur of the nutria is reddish brown. Its legs are short, and its front feet are used to hold the vegetation on which it feeds. The nutria does not use its front feet to help it swim. The rear feet are webbed and with these broad stern paddles the nutria can negotiate underwater like the expert he is. Also, he can stay submerged for as long as seven minutes.

The nutria is a practicing polygamist; one male may live, in apparent compatibility, with two or three females. The females have two litters of young a year, with four or five in each litter. The gestation period is 127 to 132 days. The young are born in the semi-darkness of a tunnel that is about four and a half feet long and nine inches in diameter.

They do not, however, stay long in seclusion. When born, their eyes are open and they have a full-length fur coat. The young nutria is scarcely twenty-four hours old before it is out in the marsh, sometimes venturing fifty or sixty feet from the home tunnel. There it feeds on the plants its parents eat, swims expertly, and takes its chances among the alligators and the gar.

Young nutria, however, like mammals everywhere, feed

largely on milk. But unlike most mammals the female nutria carries the milk in a back pack. The mammary glands, numbering four or five to the side, are arranged not on her underside but in two rows along the female's back. This arrangement permits young nutria to feed as their mother swims.

In its native land the nutria has been trapped for its fur for many decades, but efforts made there to rear nutria in captivity were never highly successful. It is believed that the first of these animals brought into the United States came to Elizabeth Lake in California in 1899 in an effort that never succeeded.

Then in March 1938 industrialist E. A. McIlhenny imported six pairs of nutria from Argentina and placed them in an "escape-proof" pen in a coastal Louisiana marsh. They prospered and multiplied.

As population pressures built up, a few of the nutria are believed to have dug out of the enclosure and waddled off to freedom in the broad marshes near by. Then came a hurricane in August of 1940. The storm flooded the marshes and an estimated 150 nutria swam over the fences.

As the nutria increased they followed the ditches, bayous, and lakes into new territory. They adapted readily. The wild marsh plants fed them well, the climate was favorable, the rate of predation on their numbers statistically insignificant, and the future bright. By September 1940, only a few months after the first nutria went wild in the marshes, workmen found one of the animals sixty-five miles away on the Lacassine National Wildlife Refuge.

In a report delivered before the twenty-first North American Wildlife Conference, U. S. Fish and Wildlife Service biologist Van T. Harris said, "Annual catch records of fur animals [mimeographed release by the Louisiana Wild Life and Fisheries Commission] give an idea of the increase of nutria in Louisiana. Severance tax was paid on 436 nutria pelts taken during the 1943–44 trapping season, whereas eleven years later [1954–55 season] the tax was paid on 374,199 pelts. The actual catch was considerably higher than these figures indicate, for many nutrias are discarded in the marsh and many are killed to protect rice fields."

Harris added the observation that the nutria had ". . . not found complete favor with most of these trappers." The trappers had already learned that in the same time required to skin and stretch a nutria pelt they could skin ten to twenty muskrats.

In 1957 William H. Adams, in a report from the Alabama Cooperative Wildlife Research Unit, placed the number of wild nutria in the United States at well over 2,000,000 animals. A survey in March 1956 indicated that in the United States nutria were in the wild in at least eighteen states, including all of the southeastern states except Tennessee.

Following the dispersal of the "swamp beaver," as the nutria was sometimes known, it was the subject of a grand-scale promotional campaign. As one South Carolina wildlife specialist said a few years later, "We were led to believe this animal would do everything but lay hard-boiled eggs." Nutria promoters claimed the animals were "four-legged weed cutters" that would quickly clear aquatic vegetation from weed-choked ponds and canals. This idea so appealed to fishermen that nutria were frequently caught and hauled to western Louisiana and eastern Texas to be released hopefully in both public and private waters.

The nutria did make inroads against the cattails, but they ate so sparingly of the thick-growing watershield and spatterdock that they did little to improve fishing, and often they turned instead to cultivated crops. But it remained for the fur-farm scheme to elevate the nutria to a new peak of imagined value.

One typical nutria farming advertisement carried in a widely circulated men's magazine in 1958 (when there were already an estimated 2,000,000 wild nutria in the United States) claimed, "New fur-bearing animal now being bred in

U.S. offers high profits to breeders. This fur is next to mink *now* in price and will soon surpass it." The claims went on to point out that nutria could be raised in any climate, with a few minutes per day of labor, and at a daily feed cost of a penny and a half per animal.

How many of their claims these promoters believed themselves is speculative. But they urged all who would to get in on the ground floor of what they predicted was soon to become a "million dollar industry."

Meanwhile, the *American Fur Breeder* magazine asked an organization called "Purebred Nutria Associates, Inc." for a statement on how many nutria breeders were in the business. They placed the nutria total at 25,000 to 30,000 in the United States, being raised by 1000 breeders, most of whom were operating in Oregon and California. Purebred Nutria Associates, Inc. also pointed out with keen foresight that "there are a lot of people being sold nutria who are going to take a terrible licking. Some of the claims being made by some of the 'unethical' sharp-shooters are criminal, such as 'Retire on a half acre,' or 'two pens in your back yard and retire.' "

They insisted that prospects were promising enough without resorting to such advertising claims. For example, they explained that a capital outlay of $4500 for breeding stock over a period of two and a half years would mean an inventory of $20,000 at the end of that period. From this you might expect a net annual return of from $4500 to $9000 from the third year on. If one wonders how they could bring themselves to let their limited breeding stock go, the explanation was revealed in their asking price for nutria, $800 for a female, $150 for a male.

Such sales organizations also talked often about mutations, and rare fur colors, which promised staggering returns. It was better than treasure hunting. The nutria mania was also reminiscent of other fur-farming schemes that had over the years dealt in chinchillas, mink, and blue foxes. Speaking of nutria, one promoter said in 1956, "Mutations, when available, sell for $1750 a pair and $3200 a trio. Under the circumstances," he added, "I honestly don't think the price charged for nutria, either Standard Brown or mutation colors, is exorbitant."

Then, as the result of a barrage of inquiries about the nutria peddlers, the Better Business Bureau, Inc. launched a study of the real value of nutria on the world fur market. One of their earliest discoveries was that, in the company of a mink or even a muskrat, the nutria wears a shoddy coat.

After its investigation, the National Better Business Bureau labeled as "false" the claims that a pair of the animals is worth $1000, that construction of a pen costs only eighteen dollars, and that overhead and feed costs were only three cents a day per animal. Also labeled false were claims that pelts were worth as much as seventy-five dollars each, that the animals were disease-resistant, that nutria fur was in unlimited demand, nutria fur garments available in all first-class stores, and that the sole reason the fur has not been more popular was because the industry had been unable to secure raw nutria pelts in the numbers needed.

And the National Better Business Bureau had a few words to add about the mutations. "It is pertinent at this point," the organization stated, "to note that a natural brown nutria can be plucked, bleached, and dyed any color of the rainbow for a few dollars."

Muskrat trappers in Louisiana marshes were then catching and sending the pelts to market. In 1956 Van T. Harris reported that "the average price of $1.50 to two dollars received for each pelt during the past several years barely provides a profit to the trapper for his share of the season's catch." Pelts of pen-reared nutria had been known to bring as much as $7.50 but the price, even for these pelts, was almost always less than four dollars each.

Investigations showed that New York fur dealers and garment manufacturers had about as much interest in nutria as they did in the armadillo. "The demand for nutria is so limited in the United States," concluded the National Better Business Bureau, "that about sixty-five to seventy per cent is exported to Europe."

Meanwhile, in Louisiana, acting chief of the state's Fur and Refuge Division, R. K. Yancey, said, "If a better price could be obtained for the pelts we feel sure that an annual yield of over 1,000,000 nutria could be derived from our coastal marshes."

Many a bilked nutria purchaser was soon face to face with stern reality. When they knew for a certainty that there was no longer hope of unloading their nutria at a profit, many who held them in captivity simply propped up the fences around the nutria enclosures and let the animals swim off into the sunset. Thus they planted the nutria in still more new territory.

By now it was widely known, too, that the nutria was guilty of more than wearing a low-value fur coat. In the early years of the animal's establishment in the marshes of Louisiana there was considerable hope, even among experienced wildlife professionals, that here would be an added resource that would not compete with the muskrat or the waterfowl to which the marshes were so important. While the nutria eat largely those parts of the vegetation sticking above the water, the muskrat eats the submerged parts as well. Some waterfowl biologists still believe the nutria can have a beneficial effect on waterfowl habitat, but there are still unanswered questions about these relationships.

Louisiana farmers were among the earliest in the United States to protest the activities of the nutria when the animals were attracted to their flooded ricefields. When the rice is small and does not provide adequate hiding cover, the nutria do their feeding after dark instead of during the customary twilight period. As the rice grows taller, however, they may move out into the fields and live there until harvest time. Harvest crews sometimes find them there and dispatch them quickly.

Like the beaver, the nutria seems attracted to moving water. Consequently, its digging is often found around pumping stations in the rice irrigation districts. The greatest damage, however, is probably done to the levees used in the flooding of the ricefields. The nutrias, either digging their own burrows or enlarging on those first dug by muskrats, frequently break levees. They have been known to cause an entire ricefield to wash out overnight.

The animals sometimes move out of their home marsh and feed in near-by fields of corn, cabbage, lettuce, and peas.

Similar damage has been reported from the nutria populations now established in Oregon, where an estimated 1000 nutria farmers were disillusioned. Many of them turned their stock loose in spite of state laws prohibiting such unauthorized releases. Oregon trappers reported catching thirty-eight of the animals in the winter of 1958–59, and three years later the total shot up to 492. But this may have been only a fraction of those killed because, as one member of the Oregon State Game Commission said, "With the furs worth only fifty-seven cents each, few trappers attempted to catch the animals."

California farmers were not long in voicing their concern about the invading nutria once populations were established in the Oakdale area in Stanislaus County. This infestation had its beginning in 1945 when nutria imported from New Jersey escaped from a fur farm four miles southwest of Oakdale. Wildlife officials were unsuccessful in wiping out the nutria once they had a bridgehead in the irrigated farm country there.

Problems created by the transplanted nutria were not likely to solve themselves. Consequently, the U. S. Fish and Wildlife Service established a nutria research station at Lafayette, Louisiana, employing a three-man research team at an annual cost of about $50,000. This little group of specialists had a single aim: to develop methods of controlling nutria damage in agricultural areas, with special emphasis on sugar cane and rice.

This is one small aspect of the imported South American rodent's effect on the American economy. In recent years demand for nutria fur has risen, and trapping of these animals has become a more profitable enterprise, bringing several million dollars a year to the Louisiana economy. In such times the nutria is viewed with much favor in the coastal regions of the state.

Meanwhile, out in the marshes, the nutria paddles about as if it has always belonged here with the muskrat and native waterfowl. The manifold ways in which it might have altered the wildlife ecology of the coastal marshes probably will not be thoroughly understood for many years.

ERRORS COMPOUNDED

Chapter 12

The Conquering Mongoose

WHEN Christopher Columbus, on his second voyage, dropped anchor off the shore of Jamaica in 1494, a mantle of green stretched from the ocean's edge up over the mountains. The tiny settlements of the Arawak Indians seemed hardly to break the continuity of the green landscape.

But while these primitive people had struck a balance with the other elements of nature, the white man would, in a few hundred years, turn this tropical island into a great cosmopolitan hodgepodge of strange organisms, wild and domestic, from all parts of the world. Like many another isolated island, Jamaica would suffer through a long list of "improvements" at the hands of well-meaning men who compensated in imagination for their lack of ecological knowledge.

Every sailing vessel that put into the harbor seemed to carry packets of seed from far-off places. Imported plants made great changes in the appearance of the island, especially during the last three decades of the seventeenth century. Captain Bligh gets part of the credit, because he is said to have imported the first breadfruit to the island. He brought it from Tahiti in 1793.

Black rats, which probably arrived with the earliest vessels, soon became pests. In fact, the rats, plus native "cane-piece" rats, led to the importation of other creatures in an attempt to eradicate them.

Rats ate sugar cane which was first grown there by Sir Thomas Modyford in 1660. By 1870 rats had become such a problem in the cane fields that one plantation owner reportedly lost one-fifth of his crop to the rodents. Meanwhile, he had paid a bounty of one penny per rat for more than 20,000 of them. Obviously, plantation owners would have welcomed any solution to the rat menace.

In 1762, Thomas Raffle thought he had found the answer in a voracious ant which was a native of Cuba. This ant *Formica omnivora* has been known in Jamaica ever since as the "Tom Raffle" ant. As nearly as modern historians can determine, the Tom Raffle ant did bite to death significant numbers of young rats. But for some reason the effectiveness of the ant diminished over the years. Plantation owners had to look elsewhere for a solution.

To complicate matters, the Tom Raffle ants became pests in their own right. One plantation owner, Anthony Davis, thought he saw the answer in a giant toad. This toad, which he called a "bullfrog," is known among scientists as *Bufo marinus*. Davis believed it would feed on young rats and Tom Raffle ants, too. Once established in Jamaica, it did eat rats and also a wide variety of insect pests.

But plantation owners never determined whether or not the bullfrog greatly reduced the ants. Their salvation, they felt, lay in finding a bloodthirsty predator that would decimate the rats mercilessly and quickly. As early as 1816 some people on the island had begun to think that the famed mongoose of India might be the answer. That year a Jamaican horticultural publication speculated that the mongoose might ". . . extirpate the whole race of the vermin."

The wonder of it is that the suggestion was not taken seriously earlier than it was. It was not until 1872, fifty-six years after the 1816 proposal, that sugar-cane growers successfully released the mongoose in Jamaica. Meanwhile, they had already tried the bloodthirsty little European ferrets.

Chiggers, however, made life so miserable for ferrets that these European predators never did establish a foothold.

Next, in the historic year of 1872, W. B. Espeut released, in his cane fields in Portland, four wild male and five wild female mongooses shipped directly from India. He watched hopefully as the first wild mongoose stock in Jamaica dashed into the rat-infested cane fields. This is an event which at the moment attracted small attention, but is now credited with causing long years of mongoose troubles that came to plague the once idyllic island of Jamaica.

The mongooses resemble ferrets or weasels in form. In India the common gray mongoose is the best known and most widely spread carnivorous wild mammal. Males average thirteen inches in length, with a bushy tail that adds another ten and a half inches. The average female is an inch or two shorter, and the adults weigh about a pound each.

The tail apparently serves several functions. It acts as a balance on the sudden darting turns the animal makes. It serves as a bedcover to supplement his relatively short fur, and it can, on provocation, make the animal appear larger than he is, as the hairs stick out when he is disturbed. The mongoose has a slender body and short legs. The nose is big and pointed, the ears short and rounded. Here is an animal excellently equipped for negotiating its way through the crevices and piles of rock and brush on which it relies for escape cover.

In Jamaica the breeding season is from January to October, with a peak production coming in March and April and again in July and August. The females usually produce two litters a year, with an average of two young per litter. Characteristically, this creature is up and about during the day and uses the night for sleeping.

The mongoose is a loner. He does his hunting by himself and sometimes engages in savage battle with others of his kind if they should meet on the trail. His favorite hunting ground is often in dense grass along streams. Studies of the mongoose in Puerto Rico, where they were introduced from Jamaica in 1877, showed that they establish a home territory 100 to 700 feet in diameter.

There are several species of mongooses, but the one chosen for the task in the West Indies is native to India, as well as Burma and Siam. In spite of what Kipling might have conditioned us to believe, the mongoose does not subsist on a steady diet of cobras. In India he can and does kill cobras, but he also takes a wide variety of other reptiles, rodents, birds, amphibians, insects, and vegetation. His choice of foods at any given moment seems to be related to abundance. Whatever is moving and is small enough or large enough, he takes. His known ability to kill snakes does not find him infallible. Sometimes snakes kill mongooses, which seems fair enough. But ordinarily the mongoose can out-maneuver the cobra and strike so fast from behind that the reptile may seem sluggish by comparison.

Once turned loose in the cane fields of Jamaica, however, the mongoose seemed not to miss the cobra of his native land. He had his work cut out for him and he went right to it. Espeut was soon overjoyed with his mongooses. In half a year his losses to rats had been cut to a fraction of what they had been in pre-mongoose days.

Word of such a miracle was certain to spread. Planters who had laughed at Espeut's idea soon wanted some of the animals to turn out in their own cane fields. When Espeut felt he did not have mongoose stock to spare, bootlegged mongooses were purchased from native poachers who trapped them and sold them. This hurried the advance of the Indian mongoose over the island of Jamaica.

Within the next few years the carnivores became established as a permanent resident, and overjoyed plantation owners shipped stock of their favorite foreign animal to Cuba, Puerto Rico, Barbados, Santa Cruz, and other favored locations. In 1882, Espeut gave the mongoose his enthusiastic approval in a paper delivered before the zoological society.

So inadequate had been the planning that few men stopped to realize that the mongoose was usually diurnal while the rats were nocturnal. In a development that should not have been surprising, the mongoose did not limit his diet to the hateful rats. While rats became the main course in his meals, largely because of their abundance, the mongoose was shortly varying his diet with birds, insects, reptiles, and amphibians.

Soon the more cautious elements of Jamaican scientific circles were entertaining misgivings about these little imported killers. In 1882 D. Morris, director of Public Gardens and Plantations for the island, wrote, "The introduction and complete naturalization of an animal possessing such strong predatory habits and remarkable powers of reproduction must have an important influence on all indigenous and introduced animals capable of being effected by it."

The mongoose in a single decade took up occupancy throughout the island. Working-class people with their little garden patches and subsistence-sized flocks of poultry probably noticed before the plantation owners did that the diet of the mongoose was indeed varied. As the rats became fewer in a locality, the mongoose turned his talents to poultry, ground nesting birds, waterfowl, lizards, and even the yellow snake which was also a predator of rats.

Shortly the native iguana was extirpated from all but remote corners of the island. Land-crab populations fell drastically. Both changes were charged to the mongoose.

Writing in the U. S. Department of Agriculture yearbook for 1898, T. S. Palmer, assistant chief of the Biological Survey, summed up the first decade of the mongoose's record in Jamaica. "Still the mongoose increased," he wrote, "and its omnivorous habits became more and more apparent as the rats diminished. It destroyed young pigs, kids, lambs, kittens, puppies, the native "cony," or capromys, poultry, game, birds which nested on or near the ground, eggs, snakes, ground lizards, frogs, turtles' eggs, and land crabs. It was also known to eat ripe bananas, pineapples, young corn, avocado pears, sweet potatoes, coconuts, and other fruits. Toward the close of the second decade the mongoose, originally considered very beneficial, came to be regarded as the greatest pest ever introduced into the island. Poultry and domesticated animals suffered from its depredations, and the short-tailed capromys, *Capromys brachyurus*, which was formerly numerous, became almost extinct except in some of the mountainous districts. The ground dove, *Columbigallian passerina*, and the quail dove, *Geotrygon montana*, became rare, and the introduced bobwhite, or quail, was almost exterminated. The peculiar Jamaica petrel, *Aestrelata caribboea*, which nested in the mountains of the island, likewise became almost exterminated. Snakes, represented by at least five species, all harmless, and lizards, including about twenty species, were greatly diminished in numbers. The same thing was true of the land and fresh-water tortoises and the marine turtle, *Chelone viridis*, which formerly laid its eggs in abundance in the loose sand on the north coast. The destruction of insectivorous birds, snakes, and lizards was followed by an increase in several injurious insects, particularly ticks, which became a serious pest, and a Coccid moth, the larvae of which bore into the pimento trees. In 1890 a commission was appointed by the government to consider whether measures should be taken to reduce the number of the animals, and the evidence collected showed conclusively that the evil results of the introduction of the mongoose far outweighed the benefits rendered to the sugar and coffee plantations."

"Recently there has been a change in the situation," Palmer added, "and the mongoose is now reported as decreasing, while certain birds and reptiles, particularly the ground lizard, are increasing. . . . Thus, Jamaica seems to have passed the high-water mark of loss occasioned by rats and by the mongoose . . . and a new balance of nature is being established."

Almost everywhere the mongoose has been transplanted,

the story has been similar; a tale of destruction. In 1883 the further importation of the mongoose into Jamaica was forbidden and a bounty was set on its head. That year, however, 215 were taken from there to the island of Hamakua in the Hawaiians, where it repeated its Jamaican performance.

The mongoose is found now on four islands of the group, Molokai, Oahu, Maui, and Hawaii. The animal finds the warm humid climate to his liking and he thrives at elevations ranging from sea level to 10,000 feet, but he thrives best below 2000 feet. He is found in the grasslands, desert scrub, and in plantations where pineapple, sugar cane, and coffee are produced. The mongoose now occupies a range covering almost 10,000 square miles in the Hawaiian Islands.

Five years after the mongoose had gotten a foothold in Jamaica, plantation owners of Puerto Rico, bent on having their share of the good things, introduced it to that island. Like Jamaican plantation owners, they were at first delighted with the results. Within a few years, however, they knew they had a biological tiger by the tail. The animals are now found throughout the island, except in deep forests and urban areas. The only safe place for a flock of chickens is said to be the dense cover beneath the cocoa trees. In the tall grasses along stream bottoms there are populations as high as one mongoose per acre.

"From 1923 to 1950," says David Pimentel of the U. S. Public Health Service Communicable Disease Center in San Juan, "the island was considered one of the few rabies-free areas in the world." Then in March 1950 there was a sudden outbreak of rabies in Puerto Rico. Public health officials began their search for the carrier, and this study, according to Pimentel's report, ". . . showed that the mongoose was the important reservoir and vector of rabies in Puerto Rico."

Records show that in 1892 the rumor spread that the United States Department of Agriculture planned to import the mongoose for release in western states where gophers were a problem in the cattle country. To those who hated gophers and knew little about the bad reputation the mongoose had already earned itself in the West Indies, this seemed a wonderfully simple answer to a complex problem. Private citizens were shortly taking steps to obtain mongoose stock.

Meanwhile, appalled scientists familiar with the ravages of this predator in both Jamaica and Puerto Rico began protesting vigorously. These importations were almost entirely prevented, but according to assistant chief of the Bureau of Biological Survey, T. S. Palmer, it was only by "the most strenuous efforts." The mongoose did not gain a foothold on the North American continent, but it came so close that naturalists were thoroughly shaken by the episode.

Chapter 13

How the Myna Went to Hawaii

ON the long list of foreign creatures men have moved to the Hawaiian Islands is the house myna, a member of the starling family, a native of India and a bird of questionable virtue once established on the islands in the Pacific. To some Hawaiians the myna bird is amusing, to some he is of no concern one way or the other, but to some he is a threat to the mental health of the human race.

The house myna is about the size of a robin. The males and females are colored alike with their black heads and necks, rich brown coloring on the back, black throat, and a white abdomen. The tail is short. The beak, legs, and feet are yellow, and there is a patch of yellow skin below and behind the eye. White flash feathers show on the wings when the myna bird flies.

Like the starling, the myna walks instead of hops and he manages this with a certain swagger which often prompts his human detractors to label him cocky and arrogant.

When busy building nests, the myna collects all manner of soft materials such as straw, paper, and cellophane and piles these together in the cavity of a tree or beneath the eaves of a building. Here the female places three or four bluish eggs which she and her mate take turns incubating for the required twelve days. Even after their young have gone from the nest the pair will stay together in the roosting trees and while walking (not hopping) on the lawns during the day.

The myna is a social creature inclined to assemble in large flocks. And although the myna bird knows a few musical notes, most of his concerts are rightfully classed as noise. When a large flock of them congregate in the giant banyan trees beside Honolulu's famed hotels, guests sometimes call the front desk with bitter complaints. They are frequently awakened at the first evidence of dawn by the chatter outside their windows. One myna bird would be interesting and entertaining to these vacationers, especially if you could escape him when you liked. But to have hundreds of them living in the trees around you is another matter, especially in view of their habit of awakening at all hours and engaging in loud and prolonged dialogue.

In years past the management of the Royal Hawaiian Hotel has conducted a running battle with myna birds. The birds use the great banyan trees around the Royal Hawaiian as roosting places. They fly off during the day to feed, but return with dusk. The first few to arrive settle quietly on their choice of the perches. But as more and more myna birds come back to the banyans they begin to jostle and crowd each other in a struggle for space and preferred roosting spots. The resulting din has spurred the hotel management on to new and often frustrating attempts to scare the birds.

One idea they tested was to tie ropes to the limbs of the trees. When the birds set up a ruckus, a hotel employee would run out and jerk on the ropes. The shaking limbs threw the myna birds off balance but accomplished little more. One hotel manager put cats into cages and hoisted these into the treetops, but reported that the birds stayed around as if to ridicule the cats.

On the mainland, meanwhile, techniques had been worked out in the war against starlings to frighten them with playbacks of their own distress calls. Would the same thing work with myna birds? It was worth a try. The birds largely ignored the distress-call playbacks. Perhaps high-frequency sound waves would cause them enough discomfort that they would leave the banyan trees. But this technique brought complaints from the hotel guests. Each time the high-frequency waves were turned on, they reportedly caused vibrations in false teeth and the switchboard lit up with calls for dental assistance. Meanwhile, the myna birds stayed on.

Why not shoot the birds? The humane society effectively blocked this. Not even BB guns were permitted against the myna birds. One hotel manager, pleading with the officials, said that even the sight of a BB gun would frighten the birds away and would it not be all right to have somebody carry a BB gun out and just point it at the myna birds? But the humane society claimed this constituted "threatening" the birds with a gun and could not be allowed.

Other ideas were tried, too. Firecrackers were exploded, but these gave only momentary aid and probably worried the guests more than the myna birds. The myna won at every turn. There was little the harassed management could do except argue that the imported birds added a tropical touch. Air conditioning permitted guests to keep their hotel windows closed and thus shut out the chatter.

The house myna was first brought to the islands from India in 1865 by Dr. William Hillebrand on the suggestion of owners of sugar-cane plantations. Sugar was a major industry and the young cane plants were being attacked by cutworms and army worms. The assignment of the imported myna birds was to devour the insect pests. They did help bring the insects under control and displayed a willingness to flock into any field infested with the cutworms. These new imports quickly created a good reputation.

Over the years in Hawaii, as ornithologists compiled a list of faults and attributes, they admitted that the myna, in addition to helping in the struggle against insects in years past, had not dispossessed any of the native species, that they were entertaining to have around, and that they could hold their own against another imported bird, the house sparrow. On the other hand, they did on occasion eat fruits, especially figs in the commercial groves.

One development the bird's importers had not anticipated was that the myna would develop a fondness for the fruit of the lantana (*Lantana camara*), a decorative tropical American plant brought into the Hawaiian Islands seven years before the first mynas arrived. The lantana fruit attracted the myna birds, which, according to the best-laid plans of men, were supposed to be eating army worms. It was soon evident that the lantana seeds passed through the mynas in perfect condition. The birds spread the plant widely until it became a serious agricultural pest. It was, in fact, possible to correlate population fluctuations of the myna with seriousness of the lantana infestations.

In fairness it must also be admitted that part of the blame for this spread goes to the turtle dove introduced to the Hawaiian Islands from China, and in recent times the introduction of an insect parasitic to the lantana has helped bring the plant under control.

How could those who first plotted its importation have foreseen that the myna would bring distress to the owners of fancy resort hotels in Honolulu or even that they would eat valuable fruit? Like so many efforts of the period to move animals about the earth, a single reason, or the search for an answer to one pressing problem of the day, was reason enough to bring in a bird or mammal and turn it out on the landscape.

In the vicinity of Vancouver, British Columbia, the related crested myna, or Japanese starling is established, and it has on rare occasions been reported from Washington and Oregon. Agricultural specialists are concerned over the possibility that it might spread still farther. It was first positively identified in the city of Vancouver in 1897. City populations have declined and it is now reported mostly from outlying areas.

About 1930 myna birds were discovered in the vicinity of Los Angeles. They were discovered in time, however, and promptly destroyed. These birds were most likely purposely imported and released. Those responsible took great risks with a potential agricultural pest. California, with its large commercial production of figs and other fruits, has little to gain from the myna bird. Many ornithologists are convinced they could easily become established there and that they would cause widespread damage.

TROUBLES EVERYWHERE

Chapter 14

Snail's Pace Accelerated

No creature, it would seem, is too large or too small to escape for long the attention of the animal transplanters. One might think that snails would be left to their own peculiar devices in their native territories. But over the years men have repeatedly given this slow-motion creature a helping hand in advancing to new lands. The snail transplanters have lavished their attentions on numerous species, in many parts of the world and for a variety of reasons.

Biologists view such efforts to spread the snail as among the most dangerous of all animal introductions. Some of the transplanted snails are serious threats to agricultural crops. Others are agents of sickness and death to human beings and domestic animals.

The most spectacular world traveler among the snails is the giant African snail, *Achatina fulica*. This one exceeds the size of a softball and weighs a pound or more.

This giant African snail was known to have eaten cocoa in Ceylon, cotton in Mauritius, and lettuce in Saipan and also to have fed on melon plants, rubber trees, legumes, and flowers. In the rice paddies it not only ate the green crop but also tramped down great areas of it. The snail even crawled up on whitewashed fences and ate off the lime. In Saipan, where efforts were made to control the snails by baiting with Warfarin, a highly effective rat poison, the snails consumed all of this rat poison they could locate and apparently relished it. Snails are also known to eat the fruit and seedlings in citrus groves.

Contrary to earlier beliefs, these creatures are not capable of self-fertilization. But a single mating can apparently assure fertile eggs from an individual female over a long period of time—perhaps for life. The giant snails are sexually mature at the age of eight months. Conservative estimates place their life expectancy at five years. Every few weeks the females deposit a new mass of 300 eggs beneath leaves or debris. This gives them an astronomical potential for leaving descendants. A little work with a calculating device reveals that in those five years a single giant African snail could have several billion descendants.

In its native territory on the African mainland and the island of Madagascar this great snail is held in check by a number of predators including insects, other snails, crabs, and a species of civet cat. In new lands to which men transported the giant African snail it was suddenly freed of these natural pressures.

In 1847 a traveling Englishman, W. H. Benson, saw these spectacular snails on a visit to Mauritius. He had an irresistible urge to take some with him on the next leg of his journey to India, and he packed a few in with his belongings. It may have been his intention to take the snails all the way home as a remembrance of his travels, but by the time he reached Calcutta he had changed his mind, and he released them carefully in the botanical gardens, where they prospered, multiplied, spread, and began competing with man and other animals for the limited food supplies.

By 1900 the big snail was firmly established in Ceylon. In Malaya it was prospering by 1928, primarily on young rubber plants. Two years later it was known to have reached Singapore. And by 1935 it was doing well in Java.

During World War II the Japanese purposely planted giant African snails on several Pacific islands to produce food for human consumption. American soldiers found the snails clinging to trees, crawling in the grass, and crossing highways. Sometimes their mashed bodies turned the roads into hazardous slippery thoroughfares.

On the Micronesian Islands, which lie east of the Philippines, the big snail has played a central role in a comedy of biological errors that has few equals in the long history of man's meddling with the world's wildlife distribution. As on many other islands in the Pacific, there was a serious rat problem. Then someone remembered that in Tokyo the giant monitor lizards seemed fond of rats.

Why not release the giant monitor lizard in Micronesia? Because, unfortunately, the lizards are up and about during the day while the rats are naturally noctural. But once the lizards were crawling about over the island it was too late to correct this oversight. The hungry lizards began feeding on chickens and eating eggs.

What would take the attention of the giant lizard away from the chickens? The lizard was known to feed on the "bullfrog," a widely traveled giant toad known as *Bufo marinus* and the same animal that had been tried in Jamaica for ant control. The big toad was introduced and the big lizards eventually turned some of their attention from chickens to *Bufo marinus*. Because this toad carries poison glands, the lizards eating them began to die off.

This should have been all right, too, except that by now plantation owners knew that the lizards were also eating grubs of the hated rhinoceros beetle, a major enemy of the coconut palm. They were also feeding on the coconut crab, which was in turn eating the detested giant African snail.

But the lizards were not the only things that ate the toads. Pigs ate them and died of poisoning. Dogs and cats, valued because they killed rats at night, caught and ate the toads—and died. Would the natives believe that the toads were guilty of killing their pets? No! They placed the blame on the giant African snail, which was meanwhile quietly varying its diet by feeding on dead cats and dogs.

This snail has been intercepted at several points on both the East and West Coasts of the United States. Authorities believe this hardy snail could adapt readily to life in Florida, Alabama, Mississippi, Louisiana, and California. The only place it has yet become successfully established in the United States, however, is in Hawaii, where it now flourishes in several locations.

The snails reached Hawaii in 1936 in the baggage of a young lady who brought two of the creatures back from a visit to Formosa. She turned them out in her garden on Oahu because she thought their brown shells marked with pure white stripes were so pretty. The snails, thus smuggled past the port inspectors, were soon inching across the countryside.

In November of the same year a citizen of Makawao, Maui, had some mailed to him from Japan. The infestations from these two transplantings were not discovered until 1938, by which time the giant snails had secured their island holdings.

Some were once sent in egg form from Singapore to Java in a tin can labeled "flower seeds." The seeds grew into snails—hundreds of thousands of them.

In 1948 a Baltimore citizen purchased one of the giant African snails from a Chicago dealer and kept it in his home for several months. The big snail escaped on one occasion, but its owner recaptured it. It was not long afterward that the snail deposited a mass of eggs. The eggs were not properly cared for and, in spite of all the snail fancier could do, they fortunately did not hatch. Specimens of this snail were kept alive in the Washington Zoo until recently. Some citizens of the United States have, from time to time, suggested that the giant snails be imported and turned out in Florida as a source of human food.

What would happen if *Achatina fulica* were to become established on the American mainland? It came close to a successful invasion, perhaps in 1946, when military vehicles were being shipped back to the United States from islands in the Pacific. Live steam was used to scald the snails from recesses of the old machines of war by the thousands. Some snails, however, still reached California alive and here again the steam treatment was rendered. So far, efforts have succeeded in keeping the giant African snail from establishing new populations in California.

While the giant African snail has, to date, failed to gain a foothold on the American mainland, less spectacular representatives of the snail family have met success. One of California's most disliked garden pests is the brown snail, which did not come to America under its own power. According to G. Dallas Hanna of the California Academy of Sciences, this snail ". . . was purposely introduced for food purposes by some of the foreign-born residents and has become thoroughly acclimatized almost all over the state. It does a great deal of damage and has been the cause of much expense, public and private, in attempts to eradicate it." It came first to San Jose about 1865, introduced by Mr. A. Delmas. It was later introduced to San Francisco and Los Angeles and, from these points, infestation spread widely. And even though it was first brought in to provide food for humans, it is rarely, if ever, eaten today.

This is but one of a lengthy list of mollusks that have found their way into California over the years, either by intent or mistake. And although most of them have failed to survive, there have been enough "success" stories, including the brown garden snail and the white garden snail, to keep California authorities jittery.

In and around many eastern cities in the United States is an attractive little snail known as the banded wood snail, believed to have come from Europe, perhaps intentionally imported by homesick immigrants. But fortunately the banded wood snail seems to be harmless and of little economic significance.

Another snail, a native of northern Europe, hardly bigger than a soybean, became known in this country as the "faucet snail" because housewives turning on their faucets would find the snails coming out by the dozens. It happened in Chicago in the summer of 1898. While snails came through faucets with the drinking water that summer, millions more of them clogged the screens on the pumphouses of the Chicago waterworks. They had to be shoveled into horse-drawn wagons and hauled away. Before many years the same snail showed up in another population explosion in Erie, Pennsylvania. No one ever established how or when or where these snails might have gained entry into this country.

Litha Spring, one of Central Florida's beautiful sparkling artesian springs, has an amazing population of foreign snails. In 1936 a Tampa dealer in aquatic supplies ordered a shipment of snails new to him, "the Philippine Horn of Plenty." They came from Pacific or East Indian islands by way of California. The dealer emptied the shipping container, then washed it near by in Litha Spring. One of these hermaphroditic snails previously mated could have been enough if rinsed from the tub into the spring. So rapidly did the horn of plenty reproduce that shortly there were 400 per square foot on the bottom of the spring. These snails were apparently free of disease and no one is the worse for their having escaped into the spring.

Public health officials are haunted by the knowledge that snails play major roles in the spread of human and livestock diseases.

Snails have long been known as hosts of flukes that cause millions of dollars in annual damages to the livestock industry. One of these, *Fascioloides magna*, the large American fluke, was first discovered in 1875, strangely enough not in North America but in Italy. Some years earlier American elk were transplanted to Italy and these animals are believed to have carried the flukes across the Atlantic to give them their start in Europe. In a protein-hungry world the widespread cattle liver fluke is a major economic problem and its control a long-time scientific challenge.

Not until World War II was the importance of the snail fully appreciated as a factor in human health. It was primarily the ill fortunes of American servicemen on the island of Leyte in the Philippines that focused attention on the seriousness of schistosomiasis, or snail fever. After a few months on the island, military personnel began to report for sick call with diarrhea, high fever, weakness, and general body pain. Shortly the military medical authorities realized that they were confronted with a major outbreak of snail fever. Before the epidemic ended, 1700 servicemen had been returned to the United States disabled. Cost for their medical treatment totaled $3,000,000 and loss to the war effort amounted to 300,000 man-days of military service. This development did, however, bring the attention of American medical science, and later the World Health Organization, to bear on the relationship of snails to human disease.

For the first time in history, men began to sense the full magnitude of the problem they faced with schistosomiasis. The disease has been known for thousands of years. The eggs of these parasites have been found in human mummies dating back at least to 1220 B.C. Even now no one has an accurate idea of the total numbers of people afflicted with the disease, but the minimum is placed at 100,000,000 and believed to be closer to 150,000,000.

The disease is prevalent in Japan, China, the Philippines, the Middle East, Africa, South America, and Puerto Rico. It was believed to have been carried to the West Indies, where it is now a serious problem, by African slaves. There are three species of these trouble-causing blood flukes, all closely related and members of the schistosomias group, each with its own native range.

The eggs hatch in water, and the larvae burrow into a host snail if they can swim to one. After about two months of incubating, they give birth to hundreds of free-living larvae called cercaria, and these are the trouble-causers. Unless they locate a warm-blooded host, they perish. But those contacting a human swimming, wading, or washing clothes in a stream or pond quickly penetrate the skin. Once they have migrated to the victim's abdomen they mature into worms and mate. They may live thirty years and produce eggs at the astronomical rate of 300 to 3000 a day.

Body wastes carry some of these eggs back into the water, and the fluke begins the life cycle over again. Most of the eggs, however, never hatch. Instead they accumulate in the spleen, bladder, and liver in such quantities that they begin to block the normal flow of body fluids and eventually cause prolonged weakness, anemia, and sometimes death.

Still another threat to human health is carried by the Thiriad snails, which are natives of the Orient. These snails are hosts for the human lung fluke which attacks the lungs and brain, causing fever, chest pains, chills, persistent internal bleeding, and sometimes death. The victim coughs the eggs up and if they fall into suitable water they hatch into microscopic larvae. These penetrate the flesh of Thiriad snails. Their life chain requires one other intermediate host, either a fresh-water crab or fresh-water crayfish in which they form a cyst that is passed on to mammals that might eat the fluke's invertebrate host. The threat carried by Thiriad snails illustrates the complexity of biological problems to be considered before the innocent-looking snail is to be transported from one part of the world to another.

Man's efforts to improve the world for his own benefit have also improved it for some snails. Big irrigation systems, designed to bring new economic health to underdeveloped areas, have often created waterways carrying snails and schistosomiasis to still more human victims. In parts of the world where snail fever is a serious health hazard, ditches of new irrigation systems are now often lined with concrete, and other precautionary measures taken to render them unsuitable habitat for snails.

Snails, as today's scientists realize, are not creatures to be turned loose nor permitted access to new regions of the world without first considering the troubles they might introduce. They cost governments millions of dollars and bring a heavy burden in human misery to millions of people. There is, understandably, constant concern over keeping such snails out of the continental United States, because scientists are convinced that the natural snail hosts of the human blood flukes could live in our warmer waters—although no one is eager to see it proved one way or the other.

Chapter 15

Newcomers to New Zealand

IN the middle of the fourteenth century, and perhaps much earlier, a fleet of great canoes moved across the seas from the north and carried a band of brown-skinned Polynesian adventurers to an island domain. From that day on, those islands of rushing rivers, blue lakes, and snow-capped peaks were marked for an endless succession of changes that would ultimately turn them into a great biological laboratory, filled with puzzles for the students of ecology.

The Maoris who beached their canoes that year, a century before Christopher Columbus was born, called this land "the long white cloud." White men would eventually name it "New Zealand." Its two major islands are about the size of Colorado, and there is no place in the country much farther than forty miles from the ocean.

The Maoris did some hunting and burning, but the changes they made were few. Until the white men came, the islands went on year after year and, except for natural changes, remained much the same as they had been for millions of years. And their natural history had been unique.

In some ancient pre-Cretaceous period of geological time, the geographers believe, a bridge of land linked these islands with areas to the north in the region of New Caledonia. But that was more than 70,000,000 years ago, and through all the intervening aeons the islands of New Zealand had lain isolated from other land masses, out of reach of visiting animals except those rare stragglers that might come by air or drift on the currents of the South Seas.

When the first men found New Zealand, the islands were covered with a lush, primitive vegetation of great variety. Groves of giant tree ferns, dense rain forests, open fields, and rocky mountain slopes existed within relatively short distances of each other. There were no mammals at all, except two species of bats. The only quadrupeds on the island, in fact, were species of reptiles and amphibians. The woodlands and fields of New Zealand had never known grazing mammals. There had been no deer, swine, wild sheep, goats, bears, cattle, or other large creatures in this land since the beginning of time. There were a few fish in the streams, a wide variety of insects, and many birds, including a dozen species which had either lost or never possessed the power of flight.

With them, the Maoris brought no herbivorous animals to disturb the natural balance. They apparently did bring along half-wild dogs, and in their canoes traveled the Polynesian rat, as well as two kinds of fleas that came uninvited and are still there to be studied by modern scientists.

Then in 1642 came the first of the white men, the Dutch captain Abel Janszoon Tasman. But the Maori discouraged any ideas Captain Tasman might have entertained about going ashore. Reluctantly he turned away from these uncharted islands which the Dutch now were to call New Zealand.

For 127 years the Maoris saw no more white men. Then came Captain Cook, whose arrival ushered in a series of changes which, in a matter of decades, would alter forever the balance of wild plants and animals.

On his second visit in 1773, Captain Cook carried three small pigs, a boar, and two sows which he turned out on the island at Queen Charlotte Sound, and these are believed to have founded the populations of wild hogs that range the South Island. They lived on vegetation and the eggs and fledglings of ground nesting birds. With each succeeding visit, Captain Cook carried seeds and animals to help make the islands more suitable for human occupation, and sealers and whalers who followed him are believed to have brought still more rats, mice, pigs, and goats.

When the regular settlement of New Zealand by Europeans began in 1840, importation of animals both wild and domestic became a major concern, first for food, later for reasons of sentiment and sport.

The disappearing forests and native wildlife led people to believe that New Zealand would, of necessity, be changed by man into a European-type landscape. Laws passed, especially during the 1860s, encouraged the importation and release of foreign species. Songbirds, for which the European immigrants seemed to harbor such a longing, were arriving frequently by ship.

New Zealand's widely known ecologist, Dr. Kazimierz Wodzicki, director of the Animal Ecology Division of the Department of Scientific and Industrial Research, has carefully studied and listed the vertebrates introduced through the various stages of man's settlement of New Zealand. According to his studies, 207 species of foreign vertebrates were brought in and released. Ninety-one became permanently established, including thirteen fish, three frogs, forty-three birds, and thirty-two mammals. Meanwhile, men were steadily altering the habitat by farming, grazing, and timbering practices.

New Zealand considers at least twenty-nine of its imported vertebrates "problem animals" today. The mistakes made by the animal importers in their haste to improve the country they found have cost vast annual sums in control measures, competition with domestic stock, agricultural crop losses, and soil erosion. The total effect on the native animal and plant populations will probably never be fully measured.

"As enthusiasm for introducing exotic animals to this country increased," Dr. Wodzicki has said, "interested persons formed acclimatization societies . . . for the purpose of procuring, liberating, and establishing any kinds of plants or animals whether native or exotic which were thought to be desirable." Acclimatization societies became important parts of New Zealand life and culture. More than two dozen still exist, although their major aims have changed. Today they are primarily hunting and fishing clubs and they work to control descendants of the mustelids, wild cats, and hedgehogs their predecessors so carefully released.

Creatures came to New Zealand from around the world. North America contributed elk, whitetail deer, mule deer, moose, Canada goose, California quail, and the bobwhite. From Europe the acclimatizers obtained the small brown owl and chamois. They turned to Asia for thar, axis deer, sambar deer, Japanese deer, chukar partridge, laceneck dove, Indian myna, and peafowl. And the long list of successfully introduced animals from back home in England included rabbits, hares, red deer, hedgehogs, ferrets, skylarks, starlings, house sparrows, and a variety of others. From Australia, 1200 miles to the west, came opossums, wallabies, black swan, Cape Barren goose, brown quail, white-backed and black-backed magpie, white cockatoo, the eastern rosella, and the laughing kookaburra. Considered together, the list made an imposing array. Considered individually, many of the species were thereafter frequently viewed as pests of astounding proportions.

Attitudes changed as damage from imported wildlife increased. By the time legislation was enacted in 1907, requiring written consent for importation of foreign animals, the damage was largely done. Importations, however, have continued.

Deer hunters in other parts of the world have difficulty visualizing a land where the red deer, England's great historic stag, and first cousin of the American elk, is classed as vermin. But in New Zealand the government offers free ammunition to those who will shoot these deer, and there are neither limits nor closed seasons. In addition, the government employs an average of 120 professional hunters to keep the deer herds under control and prevent excessive forest destruction and soil erosion.

How did the red deer get its start in New Zealand? One could hardly blame the original importers for thinking this animal would make a valuable addition to the New Zealand countryside. Here was a land of abundant and varied vegetation, favorable climate, and no large predators except man. The first deer came in 1851. A pair had begun the trip across the ocean, but the female died and the lone stag was later turned loose to bugle to his echo in New Zealand's hills. Eleven years later three more were turned out after 127 days at sea. The acclimatization societies continued to import them during the following years, usually in groups of three to eight. New Zealand's tourist department added its efforts to the deer transplanting project. Not until 1925 or 1926, when deer were already reaching alarming numbers in some regions, was the transplanting discontinued.

"There seems," says Dr. Wodzicki, "to have been almost a 'wildfire success' with regard to the establishment and spread of red deer in this country." Before many years, agriculturists and officials were noticing great damage to crops and forests and also soil-erosion damage where the deer overbrowsed.

Early dreams of the tourist department of great visitations by trophy-hunting sportsmen have been thwarted by the biological fact that, as their populations built up, the red deer have displayed what Dr. Wodzicki refers to as ". . . a steady deterioration of heads. . . ."

Meanwhile, both government-employed hunters and sportsmen pursue the red deer. Until recently there has been so little market for the meat that the carcasses were left where the animals fell. Recently, however, the export market has improved for venison. Tails, antlers in velvet, testicles, and sinews have a market value among some people of Oriental origin for their imagined qualities in restoring biological vigor in the human male.

Importers could not have foretold the great damage the deer would do. As Dr. Wodzicki has written, "It is concluded that deer are a serious menace in almost any part of their New Zealand habitat."

During the years that deer were first getting their start in New Zealand, Christian Basstian released the first opossums from Australia into the bush behind South Riverton. And the opossum liberations continued from that year of 1858 into the 1920s, when there were opossums over nearly all of New Zealand, turned out by the acclimatization societies and by trappers, all doubtless convinced they were contributing to the economic future of the country.

Australian opossums look hardly at all like the American opossum. They are all marsupials, but aside from that they have little in common. The American animal is fond of carrion and animal matter; his Australian cousins are vegetarian. The American opossum has a scaly naked prehensile tail, the Australian opossum a fine bushy tail. In fact, the American opossum by most standards is far less handsome than the Australian one and wears a fur which has historically been of considerably less value.

The reason given for the importation of the opossum in the beginning was that their fur would add another valuable resource to the land. Not only did the opossum from Australia appear valuable and harmless, he also had an appealing innocent look intensified by his cuddly appearance.

It was known that the females have but one young a year and that it spends the first several months in its mother's pouch followed by more time riding on its mother's back. Getting an animal with no more reproductive potential than this to establish sizable populations seemed to be a formidable challenge. The importers were at first greatly concerned for the safety of these thick-furred little animals.

But the opossum, relieved of natural enemies that controlled it in Australia, met the challenge. Before many years, farmers were lodging complaints, especially in fruit-growing areas, because the animal ate the leaves and also caused serious damage to the bark. Their greatest damage, however, was to broad-leaved forests. In addition to stripping entire woodlands of their leaves, the opossums moved out into surrounding gardens to feast on corn and peas. They often climb utility poles and cause power failures. The opossum is now classified as vermin and its destruction advocated and urged.

Not all the agricultural pests imported to New Zealand are big conspicuous animals. Consider, for example, the redpoll, a tiny brownish member of the finch family, so shy most people seldom see it. Most New Zealanders would scarcely believe the redpoll is common at all, in spite of the fact that ornithologists there include it in any list of the country's ten most abundant birds.

They spend the nights concentrated in central roosting areas and move out by flocks to feed during the day. Until recent times this bird was looked upon as one of the few imported birds that did not make a pest of itself. Then it became a serious destroyer of fruit and blossoms in central Otago orchards and was blacklisted with other pests of foreign origin. Control methods have included poisons, traps, and employed gunners—none of them a very satisfactory answer, according to D. Stenhouse of the Canterbury Agricultural College.

Some of New Zealand's menagerie of flying, crawling, and running creatures came to that land as the result of man's efforts to correct his former mistake. Dr. Wodzicki, in his book *Introduced Mammals of New Zealand*, has said, "The popular and still largely held belief that predators control the numbers of any population was responsible for the introduction of ferrets, stoats, weasels and cats to this country." One official even advocated bringing in Arctic foxes to eat the rabbits. He argued that there was little chance foxes would eat lambs because they had never seen sheep. For once such a plan was rejected.

The government of New Zealand imported 376 stoats and

weasels in 1883. In the following three years they released 4000 ferrets, 309 weasels, and 137 stoats. Now convinced that salvation lay with these bloodthirsty predators, the government advertised in 1888 that it would buy 30,000 ferrets. Overnight ferret farms sprang up. The ferret-stocking program ceased in 1897, but they are firmly entrenched from one end of New Zealand to the other. Neither then nor since have biologists been able to see that the ferrets made any appreciable inroads where rabbit populations were high.

Meanwhile, however, as the rabbits became increasingly serious competitors of sheep for pasture crops, the sheep farmers purchased cats in town. They fed these animals a few days, then released them to care for themselves. The cats ate rats and no doubt fed on young rabbits. They preyed on small birds and helped exterminate the native lizards. They also helped themselves to the quail, and pheasants that acclimatization societies were constantly releasing.

Upland game birds introduced, make up an impressive list of pheasants, quail, and grouse from many parts of the world. Even the American prairie chicken was given a trial when, in 1879, seventeen of these birds, *Tympanicus americanus*, from Topeka, Kansas, were turned out near Mount Thomas. There were twenty more brought in during 1881, and in 1882 another shipment of forty arrived from San Francisco. Half of these, according to the records, were stolen somewhere en route. The stolen birds never were found, and neither were those turned out in the wilds of New Zealand.

Among the twenty-five or more species of waterfowl introduced into the country were the Muscovy duck first released in 1865, the canvasback in 1905, pintail first tried in 1885, English teal in 1897, the widgeon in 1868, the gadwall in 1894, mallard from England numerous times beginning in 1867, American black duck introduced in 1905, wood duck in 1867, plus numerous times in the years that followed. The Mandarin duck was imported in 1868, the Egyptian goose in 1860, the black brant from America in 1871, the Canada goose several times beginning in 1876, the Chinese goose about the same period, white-fronted goose in 1905, snow goose (*Chen hyperborea*) 1877, Australian wild goose 1861, Australian black swan prior to 1864. With the exception of the mallard, black swan, and Canada goose, few of these ever established themselves.

The Canada goose proceeded to make a nuisance of itself. It became firmly established from a shipment of forty-eight geese released in 1905, and by 1950 most restrictions against killing the geese had been lifted because they were competing with sheep for green foods and grazing in the grain fields. Although some New Zealanders are still on the side of the goose, the big birds have never become the trophy birds they are in their native North America.

During those decades when they were busily bringing in foreign creatures to improve their country, New Zealand people neglected neither the fish nor fowl nor furred creatures. To the changes they had made in the landscape by their own farming and forestry practices, they added amazing changes by turning out foreign creatures. And, through their acclimatization societies, they maintained better records of releases than did people in some other parts of the world.

George M. Thomson, who made one of the most thorough of all studies of such importations into his native New Zealand, concluded that the story abounds in ". . . bungles and blunders." He admitted that the stocking of fish had achieved some good results, ". . . yet the record of harm done," he added, "is enormously greater."

One should not, however, assume that New Zealand has only been on the receiving end in these wildlife transfers. When citizens of Hawaii decided they simply must have some English sparrows, they turned to New Zealand where the house sparrow was already well established—in fact, like many another animal of foreign origin, it was already a serious pest.

GONE-WILD ANIMALS

Chapter 16

The Camel Brigade

IN that desert land where the Gila River flows through southeastern Arizona, the summer sun beats down with such fearful intensity that the traveler may now and again expect to see a mirage. One July day in 1875, Colonel Philip Reade, traveling through that sun-baked land, blinked and shaded his eyes against the harsh glare of the sun. There could be no doubt of it; wandering freely through the desert was a little band of Arabian camels.

There is no reason to doubt that the colonel really saw camels. For a brief period in the history of the Southwest, camels were free-roaming animals on those American deserts. How they arrived there, half-way around the world from their native soil, is one of the more unusual episodes in our long history of importing animals from distant lands. By the time Colonel Reade encountered camels on the Gila, the final chapter of the strange story was being irrevocably written.

Two decades earlier the United States Army operating in that territory faced serious transportation problems. How could you get food, clothing, and building materials to such godforsaken frontier outposts as Fort Laramie and San Antonio?

Across the country on the banks of the Potomac, the quartermaster general viewed this as one of the more difficult problems of the 1850s. Then Colonel George H. Crossman came up with a novel idea. The easy way to get freight

across the desert, he concluded, would be to bring in camels
to haul it. Why do the obvious solutions sometimes elude us
for so long? The colonel, then deputy quartermaster general of the Army, wrote a letter to his assistant, Major Henry
C. Wayne. Would the major please investigate camels?

Faced with this "request" from the colonel, the major
shortly recovered his composure and began collecting camel
literature from every available source. He heard that the
French minister in Washington had served with the French
legation in Persia and consequently was experienced in the
ways of camels. They held lengthy consultations about camels and their traits.

In the following months Major Wayne became completely
immersed in his assignment and came to see vast potential in
this plan. As Major Sidney Herbert wrote of it in 1882, ". . .
the force and wisdom of Colonel Crossman's suggestion became more clear and manifest, and he felt convinced that if
he could get a sufficient number of animals into the United
States, the camel would thrive and be as useful in this country as in Asia."

Thus fortified with facts, Major Wayne, by now the
country's best-qualified military expert on camels, was ready
for his big step. He presented the Secretary of War, the Hon-
orable C. M. Conrad, with his camel report. A significant
part of the report asked for $30,000 with which to import
the first shipment of camels from Asia. So convincing was
Major Wayne that the Secretary approved the request and
sent it up to Congress.

The man who replaced Secretary Conrad in office a short
time later was a West Point graduate of 1828 who knew
firsthand the difficulties of service on the frontier, the Hon-
orable Jefferson Davis from Mississippi. Characteristically,
Davis applied energy and tenacity in his efforts to get the
camel into the country. He ran into no trouble in the Senate,
but in the House of Representatives were some politicians
who could not comprehend the value of a camel. Year after

year the plan was tabled, and half a dozen years after he first began compiling his camel report, a despondent Major Wayne had begun to think that American legislators had permanently scuttled the "ship of the desert."

With the benefit of some masterful logrolling, however, the bill did eventually pass both houses. Friends awakened Major Wayne in the middle of the night with the glad tidings. The camels were coming!

On May 19, 1855, the elated major sailed. One year later, on May 14, 1856, he arrived back in the United States. He had sailed with thirty-three fine camels on board a Navy vessel, and arrived with thirty-four. This fact in itself appeared to many to be a good omen. The Secretary of War was so pleased with the whole affair that shortly other officers were dispatched on a second camel-buying expedition. They returned in February 1857 with forty-one camels. Three of them, lost in the rough passage, were buried at sea.

Meanwhile, Major Wayne was busy down in Texas seeing that his camels were being properly tended and utilized. He was doing his job with such thoroughness that he won acclaim from scientists both in this country and Europe. He was also commended by the Secretary of War. And in recognition of his successful introduction and acclimatization of the camel in the United States, the French *Societé Impériale Zoologique d'acclimatation de Paris* in 1858 awarded Major Wayne its "first-class gold medal."

Some officials were so excited by the potential of the project that they urged Congress to import a thousand of the beasts. Congress declined.

Meanwhile, the camels already in this country were marched off to military service at El Paso and Bowie. There they were to meet some highly prejudiced mule skinners. The troopers became convinced that a camel's habit of looking down his nose at a man is an intentional insult. Load a camel, and he may refuse to get onto his feet. Then kick him in the belly with a hobnailed boot and he may turn and spit

10. *No longer required by man, the burro was turned loose in the deserts of the southwestern United States...and thrived. Photograph by the United States Department of Interior, Bureau of Land Management.*

11. *Nearly everyone has seen pigeons, but these companions of urban man are now viewed with mixed feelings. Photograph by Edwin A. Bauer.*

12. *Enthusiastically imported for food and sport, the carp became an aquatic nightmare. Photograph courtesy of United States Department of the Interior, Fish and Wildlife Service.*

13. *For a while the only answer to rabbits in Australia was a continent-wide fence. Photographs by the Australian Geographical Society and the Australian National Publicity Association.*

14. *The often promised game bird, the coturnix, has never made it. Photograph by Edwin A. Bauer.*

15. *The reindeer, whose ancestors were turned out in Alaska to live off the tundra. Photograph by Edwin A. Bauer.*

16. *With the help of man, the opossum has extended its range from the south to other parts of the United States, including California, Washington, and Arizona. Photograph by F. M. Blake.*

17. *The colorful Reeves pheasant has been introduced repeatedly, but with little success. Photograph by Edwin A. Bauer.*

his cud into your face with uncanny accuracy. One trooper, outraged by such behavior, grabbed a club and swung wildly. The animal ducked the blow smoothly, grabbed his tormentor by the arm, and cut him to the bone with his great strong teeth. Such stories spreading from post to post did little to endear soldiers and camels to each other.

Even the army horses seemed to object to the camel odor when stabled or picketed near them. When officers explained that one camel was supposed to be worth four good mules, old sergeants only grunted contemptuously. What self-respecting professional mule handler wanted to be seen in San Antonio in charge of a string of camels?

In the four years preceding the Civil War the camels were in regular service around Camp Verde, Texas, and they became a common sight between San Antonio and the Gulf Coast. But horses were nervous around them and soldiers and civilians alike denied them affection. Officials in Brownsville even passed an ordinance forbidding camels on their streets.

In 1861 the camels fell into the hands of the Confederates. Southern horsemen looked upon the camels with disdain and promptly turned some of them loose to make their own way in the desert. A few were put to work for the Confederate Post Office Department. Union forces caught three in Arkansas and sold them at auction. There were sixty-six left at Campe Verde after the Civil War, and these were sold to a traveling man who bid thirty-one dollars each for them and took them to Mexico to be used in traveling shows.

The War Department camels were not the only ones brought into the Southwest during those years. In 1858 a British vessel brought two cargoes of camels to the Watson ranch near Houston. They were reported to be useful, but they always created too much of a sensation when they were taken to town. It seemed that you just could not ride a camel down the streets of Houston without having people stare at you.

There were also twenty Bactrian, or two-humped camels

brought from the highlands of Asia to Nevada by a San Francisco company that wanted them for hauling salt across the 200 miles of desert from Esmeralda County to the Washoe Silver Mill. But when a closer source of salt was discovered, the camels were out of a job. The last of these were used to haul cord wood around Virginia City, where citizens who chanced to look out the saloon windows might see a camel trodding the dusty streets as late as 1876.

Man spreads his ideas rapidly. Far to the north, Canadians in British Columbian gold fields heard of the introduction of camels on the southwestern frontier. In 1862 the Canadians obtained twenty-two Bactrian camels and transported them to the Caribou gold fields where they were put to work hauling supplies. The camels, however, soon proved unsatisfactory. Some were returned to the coast for disposal, but others were turned out near Westwold, where they lived off the land for several years. The last of them is believed by British Columbia authorities to have died about 1905.

The Army's grand camel experiment had two strikes against it in the years following the Civil War. Jefferson Davis, the man largely responsible for getting the camel experiment launched, was a name now unpopular among some northerners. But probably more important was the fact that the iron tracks of the early railroads were reaching into many sections of the West and putting an end to the need for cattle drives, wagon trains, and camels, too.

The most notorious of the imported camels during those years had his unbelievable exploits detailed in the pages of the *Mohave County Miner*, published weekly in Kingman, Arizona. This camel, once free from the Army, became an elusive monster of the desert. His exploits included a bizarre episode on a spring morning in 1883 along Eagle Creek.

That morning two housewives and their children had been left in their adobe house while their husbands went out on the range to look after the sheep. In her last earthly chore one of the women went to the spring for water. Her companion later told of hearing her screams. Upon looking from the door, she saw a great red monster and on it the form of a man. The animal was stomping the woman into the earth.

It was a strange story, but officials from Solomonsville could plainly see in the mud by the spring the prints of great cloven hoofs. And sticking to the bushes were bits of red hair. The beast became known through the countryside as the "Red Ghost."

During the years that followed, the big red camel occasionally panicked horses, trampled the tents of miners, and terrified hapless tenderfoot adventurers whether they saw him or only heard about him in the saloons. With each telling, the story of his exploits grew. The big camel was credited with many deeds which might have been more fairly credited to imagination and alcoholic drink.

Then one day Mizoo Hastings, looking from the window of his little ranch house on the San Francisco River, stared in disbelief because there stood the Red Ghost having breakfast in the middle of the Hastings garden. Mizoo, as calmly as could be expected under the circumstances, steadied his rifle on the windowsill and took careful aim. The Red Ghost dropped in the turnip patch.

Standing beside the fallen beast, Hastings discovered the explanation for the widespread story that the ghost camel carried a man on its back. Rawhide thongs tied so tightly around the camel that some of them had cut into his hide still held remnants of a human skeleton to the camel's back. There was a story current in those days, and perhaps true, that the Navajos had once lashed a Mexican herder to the back of a camel and chased it off into the desert.

No one knows when the last of the imported camels died, or where this occurred. Settlers sometimes reported seeing them, and it is also reported that settlers, frightened by the unpredictable free-running creatures, seldom hesitated to shoot them.

The fact that there never were great numbers of wild

camels in the deserts of the Southwest may be credited more to the forces of nature than to the care that men took with their imported animals. Few people worried about what would happen to the gone-wild camels, or how they might effect the balance of nature.

Strangely enough, the camel had its start on this continent. Its small ancestors evolved here millions of years ago and during the Pliocene and Pleistocene periods the camel's descendants found their way into South America to become the llamas of today. Others spread northward and crossed into Asia by way of the Bering Strait. They used the same land bridge followed by many species that crossed in the opposite direction from Asia to North America—the elk, bears, wild sheep, and primitive hunting men who followed them.

So the camel, thanks to Jefferson Davis and Major Wayne, made its full circle back to the land where its ancestors began the long evolutionary ascent into the modern world.

Chapter 17

Burros Among the Cacti

In 1952 the California Fish and Game Department sent to the state's newspapers what seemed to be a harmless little story. It told of burros that had for generations run wild in the deserts of southern California. The story went on to explain that there was no law protecting these feral animals. Consequently, anyone who wanted to get in some off-season shooting could hunt burros with impunity. While most outdoorsmen understandably ignored the suggestion, some did not.

"This led," said Walter S. Ball of the California Department of Agriculture, "to a few hunters taking the field, some dead burros and some very loud protests from humane organizations and interested citizens." These loud protests soon were heard all the way to the governor's office. As it turned out, that single news release designed to relieve native wildlife from the pressure of burro competition for food and water proved highly beneficial to the burro, less so to the hunters, and helped the native wildlife not at all.

Word that armed hunters were slipping through the cacti in pursuit of the appealing little burros brought cries of dismay from appalled animal lovers. Something must be done for the burros. Part-time poets published pleas in their hometown weeklies. They related how the burros' tiny feet had walked tirelessly across blazing desert sands, how the faithful little pack animals led their dying masters to water holes, and how they stood guard over the bodies of prospectors who had passed to that gold mine in the sky. No one mentioned that burros also kicked the hell out of people from time to time. One burro defender pointed out that a burro had carried Christ to Jerusalem on Palm Sunday, supposedly earning for burros forevermore a sacred status to protect them from harm at the hand of man.

In Sacramento those who held their positions at the pleasure of the voters were quick to get the message. Seven state senators put their names on a bill which would promise a year in jail and a fine of $1000 to anyone who shot a burro. When this temporary law was passed in 1953, and signed by Governor Earl Warren, a wave of relief swept the ranks of the burro lovers.

It is logical enough, perhaps, to preserve some bit of landscape where a controlled burro herd is allowed to run free, just as we do with the last of the Texas longhorn cattle in Wichita Mountains National Wildlife Refuge in Oklahoma. But emotion more than reason now worked for the burro.

California's "burro law" made it illegal to kill a wild burro in that state without a damage permit. The law later became a permanent part of the state fish and game code, and California became the only state to recognize officially the existence of wild feral burros in its deserts and give them full protection.

This was not enough. Next the burro lovers made emotional demands that the state establish a sanctuary for the animals. This measure was passed in 1957. Now the burro, whose ancestors came from Northeast Africa several centuries ago with the help of man, is considered a major enemy of native wild animals on a large area including parts of Death Valley, Saline Valley, and Panamint Valley in southern California.

Ancestors of these pampered beasts were brought originally to the desert country of the American Southwest to work. Few animals can match their qualifications for packing supplies through desert terrain. Here is a beast that can take care of itself. Prospectors led them into the most remote canyons. Mining companies used them to help haul supplies across hazardous mountain trails. As the mining industry dwindled, boom towns became ghost towns while prospectors, if they stayed in the business, turned more to motorized vehicles. If a prospector died while alone in the hills, his animals wandered off to fend for themselves. Other burros escaped. Still others were simply turned out and never rounded up, as they no longer possessed great value for man.

Any large creature that lives in these dehydrated, superheated deserts must grub for a living, and this was already true before the burros came. "When a severely limited environment is invaded by a large non-native animal with a fairly high breeding potential and no natural enemies," National Park Service research biologist Lowell Sumner has said, "new pressures on the environment are inevitable. Some native plants and animals give ground. Such an invader is the wild burro of Death Valley, a region where the severe limitations of food and water are self-evident."

Of special concern to wildlife biologists working with desert species is the native desert bighorn sheep. The bighorn has been hard-pressed to withstand the added pressures put on him by advancing human populations and he has now disappeared from much of his former range. He exists in the face of unimaginable pressures. The rare water seeps where he may come to drink at four- or five-day intervals are sometimes five, ten, or fifteen miles apart. Vegetation is scarce between the watering holes. Now in some areas he must share his scant supplies of food and water with the burros.

In a report called the *Status of Feral Burros in California*, the state Department of Fish and Game has said, "On the lower western slopes of the Panamints and in Butte Valley, the better browses have been killed out, and low value plants such as white bursage are nearly gone. The burros are now heavily utilizing creosote bush. The foliage of this plant is rarely taken by any animal. Utilization of creosote bush reflects a very severely depleted range condition. Old timers tell of former high numbers of bighorn sheep in the Panamints. At present a very low population exists. In the summer of 1955 during a partial survey of the western slope and main ridge of the Panamints for wildlife species, more than 25 burros, one bighorn and fresh tracks of three other bighorn were observed. From examination of the serious damage wrought to the range by burros, it seems safe to assume that they have been the chief cause of the large reduction in bighorn numbers in this area.

"The most serious aspect of range plant depletion in desert areas," says the report, "is the extremely slow recovery rate of native vegetation." Even under complete protection from the foraging burros, the desert vegetation might require several decades to return to its original condition.

In Death Valley in 1935 the National Park Service began detailed studies of the relationships of wild burros to the desert bighorn. Over the next twenty-four years the situation was observed by five park rangers, a park naturalist, six park biologists, and eight biologists from other co-operating agencies. Their testimony was in agreement; where the burros have increased noticeably, the bighorn have dwindled or disappeared. Those watering places where good populations of bighorn still come to drink seem to have one characteristic in common—there are no burros there.

The burro is at best a difficult creature to get along with around a water hole. He wants to be king. "The burro is the dominant creature on most of his range," says game manager Richard A. Weaver of the California Fish and Game Department, "and the competition for water in areas of limited supply is acute." In seeps where the water supply is low, burros can consume the entire amounts. In larger water holes they frequently foul the water and render it unusable. They are also known to chase away other animals, especially desert bighorn ewes and lambs. They make life difficult as well for the domestic stock that might rely on the same watering holes. Burros have even been known to break water pipes with their hoofs and cause water to spill out on the ground before it can reach holding tanks.

The major populations, or "infestations," as some wildlife biologists prefer to call them, of feral burros today are in California, Arizona, Nevada, and New Mexico. They are, however, running wild in every western state except Washington and Montana. It should not be assumed on the basis of this, however, that the feral burro is about to overrun the land. The best estimates of total wild populations in 1957 placed the number below 13,000. But these animals are scattered over rugged, remote, and unproductive regions where a single large animal can make a serious added drain on food and water supplies.

"The areas surrounding water holes," says the California Department of Fish and Game, "are often completely devegetated through trampling and feeding by burros. This causes the water hole to become unattractive to birds and small mammals as the cover is needed for nesting, roosting and protection.

"In some instances burros have not only ruined a spring, but have torn up the improvements made there. The small water supply at Thumb Rock Spring in the Providence Mountains was improved by a Department of Fish and Game crew by installing a plastic pipe to carry water to a concrete basin. Burros tore up the pipe and trampled it and smashed the concrete basin."

Cattlemen report that wild burros sometimes fight with cattle around watering troughs, and the jacks have killed calves ". . . by rearing up and smashing down on their backs."

For the sake of our native wildlife on the western deserts, some control measures over the self-reliant burros are essential. The desert creatures live in a world of harsh reality, and the recently arrived burros inflict added, and often unbearable, burdens on them. This is a problem that calls for solutions based on biological principles. Sentiment for the burro—the stranger in the desert—is responsible for hardships on all the creatures living there, the burros included.

Chapter 18

Pigeons Everywhere

FOR countless centuries the common pigeon has been man's close companion. Beloved by poets, philosophers, young lovers, old lovers, and those who had messages to send, the pigeon flies about us on muffled wings and coos with warmth and affection. What the pigeon does not realize is that men trust him less than they once did, because they have found him to be a carrier of serious human ailments. In city after city pigeons are no longer welcome in the church belfry or on the statues of the founding fathers. This is sad in a way, for the pigeon has been a long time among us.

Those inclined to defend the pigeon can compile a lengthy list of his accomplishments and traits of good character. For thousands of years before telephones and radios, pigeons carried messages of great news and intrigue. It was a pigeon who first took the news to Rome that Caesar had conquered Gaul. When the first news reached Paris of the sad fate of Napoleon at Waterloo, it was carried by a pigeon. During World War II underground forces in occupied France dispatched pigeons to the British Isles with the latest intelligence, while German commanders stationed their best shotgunners along the coast to intercept the messengers.

One medical center near Washington, D.C., recently worked out a system to equip its doctors with pigeons as they went out on calls around the city. If the doctor should need rapid diagnosis of a body fluid, a vial is strapped to a bird's leg and the pigeon is off to the loft on the clinic roof. And he gets there faster than an automobile could make it in this age of congested traffic.

Meanwhile, in Formosa, an artificial cattle-breeding association flies frozen cattle semen to its technicians back in remote mountain regions. The early leg of the journey from the United States is by great powerful jet planes. But when the semen must be transported into the rugged mountain hollows, pigeons get the job.

Even if it were not for such practical applications of this bird's homing abilities, those who defend the pigeon would still find much in its favor. They would explain that squabs have provided choice eating for humans for ages and that the raising of them is still a big industry. They would tell of the pleasure derived from racing pigeons, and of the entertainment flocks of pigeons in the park bring to the lonely. And what of his reputation as the symbol of love and brotherhood?

Little wonder that men, having convinced themselves through the centuries that the pigeon is one of Nature's rare good gifts, should take the birds with them wherever they moved to new lands. The common street pigeon traces his ancestry to the rock doves, natives of the temperate regions of Europe and Asia. They were first domesticated nearly 5000 years ago. The pigeons first came to North America with early settlers; the exact date is lost. The first rock doves on these shores were domestic stock. Historians believe the pigeon may have been the first domesticated bird. Once the pigeon is loose in the wild, he soon reverts to his historic color and shape, but while he may no longer be a captive of man, he does not desert the haunts of man.

Throughout the world the family of pigeons and doves contains 289 different species. They are, characteristically, birds with small heads, short necks, and stout bodies. Their beaks are short, and in the world of birds their method of drinking is almost unique because they suck water through their beaks as if equipped with a sipping straw. On the ledge of a building or the rafter of a barn the pigeon puts together a shallow pile of sticks where the hen bird deposits two eggs. The pigeons divide the chore of incubation. Young pigeons develop rapidly and within two or three weeks after hatching are ready to leave the nest and sit on a statue in the city park. Meanwhile, the old birds start another brood. Pigeons quickly increase their numbers and spread to new territories.

Until fairly recent times, city fathers sent crews out to clean up behind the pigeons and, aside from the fact that it was a nuisance, they did not give much thought to the problem. It was simply one of the requirements for running a clean city.

Shortly after the end of World War II, however, medical scientists began to trace cases of psittacosis, or parrot fever, directly to pigeons. At the University of California, Dr. Karl G. Meyer made laboratory tests of the pet pigeons of a parrot-fever victim. A large percentage of these pigeons carried the responsible virus. In New York, Massachusetts, Minnesota, and California, still other cases of psittacosis were being traced to pigeons. At least two fatalities resulted from these. Now that we know that the disease can be carried by pigeons, ducks, and other birds as well as parrots, it is usually called ornithosis.

Shortly afterward there was an outbreak of pigeon-carried psittacosis in Philadelphia. Investigators found that pigeons in all parts of the city were spreading the virus in their droppings. There followed a control campaign in which 10,000 Philadelphia pigeons were killed within a year.

Next, during the winter of 1944–45, officials in Chicago, seeking the cause of a growing number of parrot-fever cases there, traced the disease directly to the city's large pigeon population. According to findings by the city's Board of Health, about forty-five per cent of Chicago's pigeons carried the disease. Other cities became equally concerned. There were 563 cases reported in 1954 and officials suspected that numerous other cases of parrot fever were mistakenly identified as virus pneumonia.

Then a frightening new development prompted health officials to become still more concerned about their pigeons. At the annual assembly of the Medical Society of the District of Columbia in November 1964, a team of researchers from the U. S. Public Health Service indicted the pigeon as the carrier of one form of meningitis. This brought into the open a discussion that had been going on in research circles and public health laboratories for many years. It was known that the fungus *Cryptococcus neoformans*, causing cryptococcal meningitis, can be inhaled with dust containing particles of dried pigeon manure.

Records showed there were two deaths in the United States in 1964 attributed to this disease and traced to pigeons. In one year eleven city workmen in Cincinnati became ill after cleaning the pigeon manure out of an abandoned tower in Eden Park. One of the workers died, probably from the cryptococcal meningitis or from pigeon-carried histoplasmosis. The city fathers promptly began to enforce the anti-pigeon feeding law because much of the pigeons' increase over the years has been attributed to the kind-hearted spreading of feed for the birds.

Across the country, in city after city, the pigeon came under suspicion. Dr. Chester Emmons of the U. S. Public Health Service had said, "Old pigeon droppings constitute the only source so far where we can consistently find the fungus in large numbers. . . . We believe such droppings constitute a potential public health problem."

Two years earlier New York City's Department of Air Pollution Control revealed before the Air Pollution Control Association at its annual meeting in Chicago that its scientists had actually calculated the amounts of dried pigeon wastes floating in the air of New York City. Said the report, "New York City air definitely contains significant amounts of dried pigeon fecal matter." It has been computed that a citizen of New York City inhales three micrograms of pigeon dust daily.

Nor does the list of diseases carried by pigeons stop here. A common fungus-caused disease known as histoplasmosis is carried in pigeon droppings and can result in high fever, lesions of the lungs, and enlargement of the liver and spleen. Chicken mites that normally live on the blood of young pigeons may kill their avian hosts, then turn to human hosts. If they bite human beings, they cause severe skin ailments. An expectant human mother infected with toxoplasmosis may pass the disease on to her offspring, causing blindness, brain damage, and usually an early death. The parasite causing the disease is found in pigeons. Pigeons are also known to carry the virus that causes encephalitis, which attacks the brain and nerve tissues of humans, and which mosquitoes carry from birds to man.

There are many ways to fight back at pigeons, including shooting, trapping, poisoning, destroying their nests with long-handled hooks, and cleaning up their feeding areas. But each of these arouses the protective instincts of the pigeons' human benefactors. Consequently, the city officials fighting pigeons often pursue the birds in the wee hours of the morning when the populace sleeps.

Some months ago Paris officials decided something had to be done about the pigeons. First came a law making it illegal to feed pigeons around Notre Dame Cathedral, the Opéra, and other public buildings. It was hoped this would encourage pigeons to forsake city living and move out to the country. Then every Tuesday and Saturday morning, crews of pigeon catchers slipped out before daylight and set up a great net. The birds caught in these baited stations were crated and carefully trucked to a village 124 miles away, where for several days they were given good care, then released, whereupon many of them immediately exercised their famous homing instinct and headed back to town.

Through the centuries the pigeons flew about man's cities and roosted. Wherever men moved to new lands the bird was soon in evidence. Considering the fact that they eat the farmer's grain, harass the city pedestrian, and carry sickness and death, it might have been wiser by far if the pigeons turned out to establish wild populations in new lands had been wrung by the neck instead.

SURPRISE PACKAGES FOR SPORTSMEN

Chapter 19

Wonder Fish from Europe

WHEN Rudolph Hessel came down to the harbor on that morning in the winter of 1876–77, he realized that, for the moment at least, he had done all he could. But he could not put aside his concern and apprehension. As a fish culturist for the United States government, he had been dispatched to bring back a shipment of what he firmly believed to be the world's finest fish. He saw his mission as one of vital importance to the United States.

But there was sadness in Hessel's heart on the day of his return. That was a rough winter on the North Atlantic. Frigid sweeping winds howled around the ship in which Hessel and his fish had ridden the pitching waves. The crossing had been difficult for man and fish alike, and it might have been that the fish rolled back and forth too roughly in the tank. When his boat dropped anchor in Boston, Hessel, chagrined and long-faced, walked down the gangplank knowing his mission had failed. All his wonderful fish had died.

Hessel, however, was not one to give up easily. He acquired early passage back to Europe and at Höchst near Frankfurt purchased another lot of fish—all vigorous and especially selected. Then on May 26, 1877, he landed at New York. His fish—all 345 of them—were frisky and well. Hessel lovingly installed his treasure in ponds in Boston's Druid Hill Park, then rushed down to Washington to receive the applause of a grateful Congress. It was the carp, of course,

that Rudolph Hessel introduced into this country in his conviction that it would quickly outclass our native species.

Two hundred and twenty-seven of Hessel's carp were the
popular partly scaled mirror variety. The other 118 were the
scaled carp destined to dominate so many square miles of
American waters. When it became evident that the carp were
overcrowded in Boston, Congress itself quickly took up the
problem of what to do about them. That staid body rose to
the need of the hour and appropriated $5000. Instructions
were then issued to use this appropriation to put Babcock
Lakes in Monument Park in Washington, D.C., in shape to
accommodate the immigrant fish.

The following spring these lakes in the nation's capital
were ready. Sixty-five leather carp and forty-eight scaled
carp were carefully transferred from Boston to Washington
and released in their new homes. The patient and determined
Hessel, his mission accomplished, stood on the bank and happily watched his charges swim off into the water. From
here on, it was up to the carp.

By now, people in many parts of the country were practically lining up to get breeding stock of these wonderful fish.
Congressmen haggled to see that their own districts got their
just deserts. In 1879, 12,265 of the new fish were happily
spread out over twenty-five states and territories. And the
fever spread. Everybody wanted to share in the good things.

In 1883, 260,000 carp were divided among 298 congressional districts. Only three congressional districts were left
without carp that year. But soon there would be enough carp
for everyone. "Almost every farmer," said one fish specialist, "wants a carp pond in his front yard, back yard or barn
yard."

Typical was Nevada, where carp were imported because
of a promise H. G. Parker, the state's first fish commissioner,
made to the Nevada legislature in 1879. "Should the appropriation be made," Parker said, "my first expenditure
therefrom will be for the introduction of eels and the veg-

etable-eating carp; the latter a German fish and the most delicious of all known fishes." Persuaded by this plea, the legislature voted favorably and in two years Nevada planted carp in a hundred places throughout its limited waters.

Soon reports of the carp's fine progress were filtering back to Washington from widely scattered parts of the country. From New York on April 4, 1884, E. G. Blackford wrote to U. S. Fish Commissioner S. F. Baird to tell him that in a barrel of shad arriving that day at the fish market from the James River in Virginia was one German carp, ". . . weighing three and a half pounds."

From Savoy, Texas, Baird received a letter in which Samuel Johnson told how "My carp which you sent me the 10th day of January last are doing well. They grow like China pigs when fed with plenty of buttermilk." Johnson added that he fed them on table scraps and that, while they liked "biscuits the best," they ate everything he offered them. He even had them trained to come to the rattle of a sheep bell at feeding time. "I wouldn't," said Johnson, "take $100 for them."

Before long, spring freshets and flash floods washed carp out of their ponds and set them free to explore new worlds and populate new waters across the country. "German carp are nomadic in their habits," wrote Edward Prince after observing them during their first fifteen years in Canada, "and wander apparently aimlessly into all accessible waters, hence if introduced into any streams will spread rapidly over the whole system."

For a few years this did not worry anybody much. If the carp was really as good as its advance publicity claimed, people everywhere could soon share the benefits of Hessel's work.

But the days of unstinted praise for this immigrant fish were soon to end. Within a few years, everybody, absolutely everybody, had all of this kind of fish he needed. There came the first murmurings of a strange reaction against the carp;

shortly this dissatisfaction began to sweep the country. Here was a reaction which Hessel had not anticipated. Neither had the politicians who helped promote the carp scheme in the beginning. The novelty of the immigrant carp, the fish that was said to be everything a fish should be, was wearing off.

Those states that had hopefully turned carp loose in public waters to enhance the angling prospects within their boundaries were greatly disappointed. Sport fishing in many places became less and less productive to the angler. Serious ecological studies would probably have shown that gradual warming and pollution of the waters were partially responsible for some of the poor fishing. But this was not easily explained and perhaps not fully understood in those times. Anglers looking around for a scapegoat centered their attention on the imported carp. They pronounced him guilty of eating fish, consuming spawn, muddying the waters, rooting up wild rice, being low in food value, and, perhaps most seriously of all, they accused him of not being a game fish.

Just as they did in other places, the carp had prospered in Nevada. By 1895 the fish commissioner was George T. Mills, who was viewing the fish with alarm and disgust. Did he blame his predecessor, H. G. Parker, who had labored to import the carp? Not exactly. Commissioner Mills put it this way: "Several years ago, during the carp furor, the general government, while not entirely to blame, was 'particep criminis' in foisting upon this state, and in polluting our waters, with that undesirable fish, the carp. True, applications for same were made by many of our citizens, ignorant of the qualities and habits of the fish and unsuspecting as to the ruin their introduction would bring. Time has now established their worthlessness, and our waters are suffering from their presence. As a food fish they are regarded inferior to the native chub and sucker, while their tenacity to life and everlasting hunger give them a reputation for 'stayers and feeders' unheard of in any fish reports I have seen up to date. A resident of Humboldt," the commissioner joked, "informs me they have not only devoured all the fish food in the Humboldt River, but also the duck food and a band of sheep ranging along the banks."

The carp, oblivious to the furor he was causing, went right ahead advancing into new waters and rapidly populating additional lakes and streams with his kind. Soon politicians again began to feel the pressure. By 1900, commercial fishermen on Lake Erie were appealing to the government to make a study of the carp, or, as some commercial fishermen still called it on eastern markets, the "Great Lakes salmon."

Obviously the time had arrived for man to make a valiant effort to correct a mistake which he had, in his vast ignorance of ecology, made. Consequently, in the summer of 1901 the United States Commission of Fish and Fisheries assigned Dr. Leon J. Cole, a brilliant young biologist, to ". . . investigate the habits of the carp and gather any information available relative to its usefulness or its obnoxiousness."

Dr. Cole centered his research project in the waters of Lake St. Clair where there were, by that time, serious complaints against the imported fish. Newspapers were quoting fishermen on the subject. "An old fisherman who has plied his trade on Lake St. Clair three miles above Mt. Clemens for 23 years," one paper reported, "says in three years more there will be no fish except carp left in the lake. The carp eat the spawn and destroy the perch, bass and other good fish in those waters, and the supply is already much reduced." He suggested, according to the newspaper report "that the government offer a bounty of three cents or so for the destruction of the carp in order to save the other fish."

Through three summers Dr. Cole investigated the carp's habits and searched for a weak point in its life cycle. But he must have known even then that he was fighting a losing battle. He studied the carp and came to understand it well. He found no weak link in its life chain where men might attack it. He then reached a sensible conclusion which has not yet been seriously challenged. Summed up, his findings were that carp are here to stay, so we may as well relax and accept the fact.

This fish has done little that is beneficial to the native waterfowl that were here before he arrived. Waterfowl numbers have fallen drastically in recent times. As much as we might like to, we cannot give more than a fraction of blame to the carp or ignore the drastic effects of drainage, overshooting, lead poisoning, and competition for space. Does the carp escape free and clean of all blame for the troubles that have beset our native ducks and geese? Not quite.

Before the carp arrived on the American scene, many lakes had changed little in recorded history. One of these was Lake Koshkonong in Wisconsin where great clouds of canvasbacks dropped from the skies to feed and rest en route south for the winter. The big attraction for these magnificent ducks was the wild celery and the pond weeds. "When morning broke," said one writer of the 1870s, "the water was covered with these beautiful birds as far as the eye could see."

Then came the carp plague. These fish were introduced into Koshkonong in 1880. Their population explosion was typically spectacular. The big fish multiplied magnificently and went rooting and grubbing around the lake bottom with startling vigor and efficiency. Soon the wild celery and the pond weeds were gone and so were the canvasbacks.

The same thing happened to numerous other canvasback lakes; they exchanged their waterfowl for carp. In the fertile shallow waters of western Lake Erie, once among the country's finest hunting grounds for canvasbacks, the carp made quick work of the wild rice and wild celery.

"Changes in aquatic habitat," as pointed out by Jerome H. Kuehn and John B. Moyle of the Minnesota Department of Conservation, in the U. S. Department of the Interior publication *Ducks Tomorrow*, "come quickly as a carp population builds up. As the fish multiply, weed beds decline. Thick growths of pondweeds, water milfoil, coontail, and other plants are replaced by bare mud. Water that used to be clear becomes cloudy with silt. . . . Their [carp] removal often brings a spectacular clearing of the water and improvement for waterfowl."

As the water is roiled by the rooting carp, light penetration is reduced. This cuts down the growth of submerged plants, including some most important to waterfowl. It is believed that this carp activity brings nutrients up from the bottom of the lake and that these nutrients in solution increase the growth of blue-green algae. And these, in turn, cause a further decrease in light penetration.

Few states have ever taken extensive direct action to combat the carp. One exception is Wisconsin, which in 1934 established one of the most involved fish-control programs ever attempted against non-game fish. The Wisconsin Conservation Department maintains five stations in its frustrating efforts to control rough fish in the southern part of the state. From these centers go crews of carp catchers equipped with nets, boats, barges, automatic loaders, and other modern equipment pursuing descendants of Herr Hessel's beloved carp. In a single day one of these crews may set and take up a seine three-quarters of a mile long. When winched in out of the lake, it may hold 100,000 pounds of fish.

Game fish are quickly removed from the net and flipped back into the waters. Carp are loaded on trucks and hauled away to be sold to fur farmers for mink feed for as little as one and a half cents a pound.

Each year Wisconsin state crews, as well as others working under contract, remove some 6,000,000 pounds of rough fish from the water, including large numbers of sheepshead. In recent times the annual cost of rough-fish control has been $300,000. Sale of the fish returns half of this amount, leaving an annual cost of $150,000. Figured from the year the program began in 1934, this would come to $4,500,000 spent by Wisconsin people on a program for which the carp was responsible. Actually, because fish-netting efficiency has improved, the total cost is believed to be higher than this figure.

"Every year," said one worker in the Wisconsin Conservation Department recently, "greater demands are being made by interested sportsmen to remove more carp from infested waters and allow more room for game fish."

Meanwhile, there is a nagging conviction among some fish ecologists that such projects waste money and nurture futile hopes. They cite the natural propensities of the carp to replace itself. Its biotic potential is staggering. Supposing, for example, that in a small carp-infested lake the fish-removal crews could schedule one day a year for rough-fish removal. (Many Wisconsin lakes are seined only once in three years.) They set their big seines and make their wondrous haul, and the carp they take out of that lake are a sight to behold! On the banks stand half a dozen local fishermen smiling broadly. Now the fishing is being improved.

But the carp is winning this contest, too, because the seines cannot be worked into every corner of most lakes. The carp cannot all be removed by seining and Wisconsin authorities readily admit this. "When first initiated," says a Wisconsin bulletin explaining the rough-fish control work, "plans called for elimination of carp and other rough fish. Now everyone realizes this is an impossible objective except in poisoned-out lakes." University of Wisconsin fisheries biologists found in tests that carp have a tendency, when frightened, to mass together on the bottom of the lake, and that the seines often glide right over these piles of fish. They also found that carp become trained at escaping the nets and that once they find an exit they use it if repeated efforts are made to catch them in the seines.

Always there are some carp left. And a single fifteen-pound female that eludes the nets may drop half a million eggs.

Recent studies have also shown that heavy seining may

create drastic changes in the age classification of carp populations in a lake, with a higher percentage of young carp following the seining. In one such test juvenile carp, which were known to make up thirteen per cent of the population before seining, composed ninety per cent of the population following seining.

Why is this significant? The explanation lies in the differences in foods consumed by carp of different ages. Minnesota fisheries research has shown that young carp are big consumers of aquatic insects, which are highly important foods in the diets of game fish and waterfowl. Consequently, the fish seiners, by removing the old carp and leaving room for young ones, may be working against native wildlife.

One solution in smaller lakes is to kill off all the fish and begin over. But, even so, such ponds have a way of being reseeded to all manner of undesirable fish by visiting anglers, small boys, and flash floods.

The one carp-control possibility that looms hopefully on the horizon is the work to develop a selective chemical that will kill carp, yet prove harmless to other fish. This is now being investigated in research projects of the U. S. Fish and Wildlife Service in a laboratory at La Crosse, Wisconsin.

Meanwhile, each passing spring brings from state fish and game departments the old feeble suggestion that fishermen get out there and catch those carp. In spite of the fact that the carp is not a good game fish and hardly a gourmet's delight, these plaintive entreaties continue. But one can hardly blame the fish managers for urging sport fishermen to catch carp. So far, there is little else to be done about them.

The carp is a scourge and without friends. But he is a roughneck among fish and no matter how we combat him his future looks secure. As Rudolph Hessel promised, the carp adapted readily to American waters.

Chapter 20

The Unlovable Rabbits

In 1954 a Columbus, Ohio, newspaper reported, "The European rabbit, which has ravaged Australia and New Zealand, has been recently introduced into Ohio and Pennsylvania by sportsmen." The report was true. Beagle clubs and rabbit hunters in several states were then importing and releasing European rabbits to improve the quality of their sport during the coming autumn. Several state game and fish departments were caught by surprise; then farmers and public officials began to awaken to the frightening possibilities of this development.

The ability of the European rabbit to adapt to life in new territories has enabled this three-pound mammal to bring devastation to many different areas of the world. In 1903 rabbits were taken to Laysan Island in the northern part of the Hawaiian group. Eventually their descendants ravaged the vegetation on the island, reducing the known list of twenty-six species of plants to four and causing the disappearance of several birds that had formerly occupied the island. It caused the near-extinction of the Laysan duck and the Laysan finch-bill. Laysan was turned into a desert. One hundred and fifteen miles to the west, rabbits from Laysan were turned out on Lisianski Island, where they stripped the island of its vegetation, then starved to death. Similar wildlife tragedies have stalked the European rabbit elsewhere that people released them.

One of the most involved and unpredictable sequences of events in the history of rabbit transplanting was reported by the French naturalist Roger Heim. Rabbits were introduced to the Macquarie Islands, far to the southwest of New Zealand, to provide food. They were shortly competing with sheep, however, and farmers began looking about for a cure for the rabbit problem. The cat appeared to hold promise. So cats were turned loose to eat the rabbits. But the cats turned to eating sea birds. This was bad because sea-bird eggs were an important food for the native people.

The cure for the cat appeared to be the dog, so dogs were turned loose. To the surprise of the planners, however, the dogs neglected the cats in preference to the seals, also an important source of human food. There was little the wildlife manipulators could do then except admit that the dogs had not controlled the cats that had not controlled the rabbits that seemed so desirable in the beginning.

On small islands the rabbit's spread was limited by saltwater barriers. Where the animal could become established in larger areas, such as New Zealand and Australia, it has marched across the land like a plague, altering entire economies, destroying agricultural enterprises, and changing the lives of human populations. Instance after instance could have been paraded out to demonstrate the folly of turning these animals out on the mainland of North America in the 1950s. But Pennsylvania sportsmen alone released an estimated 7000 of them, Ohioans introduced several thousand, Indiana about 500, with Illinois, New Jersey, Wisconsin, and Maryland also involved.

Some officials believed their states were protected from such invasions by the Lacey Act of 1900. This law had forbidden importation and release of any foreign wild animal without a permit from the Secretary of Agriculture. But the rabbit importers had an answer for this one. These rabbits, they insisted, could not be excluded as foreign animals because they were being trapped and shipped from the San

Juan Islands in Puget Sound, quite definitely a part of the United States. Faced with the biological reality of a serious animal invasion, the officials were momentarily stumped by a geographical technicality.

Several of the islands in the San Juan group have in times past been stocked with rabbits of foreign descent, including San Juan Island, Long Island, and Smith Island, where the rabbits engaged the United States Navy in an historical battle. Wildlife specialists in the Washington State Department of Game insist that the animals on these islands today came not from wild stock, but from domestic rabbits that reverted to the wild.

Smith Island, lying at the entrance to Puget Sound, was occupied at the turn of the century by the Navy Department, which operated a radio compass station there, and also the Department of Commerce, which maintained a lighthouse station. In addition, the Department of Agriculture administered Smith Island as a bird refuge, especially for the protection of the puffins, murres, and other sea birds that had long nested there.

Rabbits first came to Smith Island about 1900 when the keeper of the lighthouse decided their meat could be sold in Seattle and thus supplement his income. He took to the island an unrecorded number of domestic rabbits, descendants of common European rabbits, *Oryctolagus cuniculus*, already infamous in other parts of the world.

But the lighthouse keeper had no thought of turning his rabbits loose to forage for themselves. He installed them in cages. Later he imported new stock to prevent inbreeding. Eventually, however, he was replaced by another lighthouse keeper, and the new attendant, unattracted to rabbits and seeing little promise in them, opened the cage doors and turned them out.

In the following years the small contingent of Navy personnel operating the radio compass station watched the advance of steadily increasing rabbits with alarm. By 1924 the rabbits' food supply was running low. More disturbing to the sailors was the fact that the official Navy buildings now leaned strangely to one side or the other. They were undermined with rabbit tunnels. The powerful U. S. Navy, unable to cope with the rabbits, sent an S.O.S. to the Biological Survey, and in May 1924 the Survey dispatched two biologists, Leo King Couch and Theodore Scheffer, to the Navy's rescue. The desolate sight confronting them on Smith Island told the biologists a distressing story.

By now the green vegetation that had once blanketed the island was almost gone. Rabbit burrows were so thick that a man had to step carefully around them when crossing the island. So completely had the rabbits tunneled that the banks were caving in along the shore; rabbits were literally reducing the size of Smith Island.

"We saw evidence of rabbit depredation everywhere," Couch later wrote in the *Journal of Mammalogy*, "and animals . . . running in all directions." It was his conclusion that ". . . destruction of forage and shrubbery no doubt accounted for the lack of nesting birds." On this island, where birds had formerly assembled and nested in great numbers, Couch now found two robin nests, some tufted puffins present along the bluffs, but not nesting, and one "emaciated" California murre wandering alone among the bracken ferns. Even the rabbits, undernourished now, were in poor condition and diseased.

The two investigators decided that the dry month of August would be the most suitable time to attack the rabbits of Smith Island. They organized crews, made plans, and on the appointed day they dropped slices of apple dusted with strychnine alkaloid along the rabbit trails.

The next morning they picked up 621 dead rabbits. Then, to kill rabbits that had taken refuge in the burrows, they spent the remainder of the day forcing calcium cyanide dust into the tunnels, where the chemical reacted with moisture to form cyanogen gas. After eight days of this effort, few rabbits were any longer seen on Smith Island. And these, according to Couch, ". . . appeared extremely wild."

Those few, unfortunately, were still left for seed. In addition, stock had been transferred years before to other islands in Puget Sound. It was from these sources of "gone wild" rabbits that states later obtained stock for their unofficial and hazardous stocking of San Juan rabbits.

It would have seemed to the most casual observer by this time in the middle of the twentieth century that the biological risk involved was tremendous. Here was a highly adaptable animal that had repeatedly demonstrated its natural ability to survive all manner of persecution and lay waste vast new areas. Unlike the North American cottontails, these European rabbits also do extensive damage by burrowing. Their burrows become a hazard to livestock, cause soil erosion, and complicate the chore of fighting the rabbits.

The ancestry of this rabbit is traced back to Spain and North Africa. The conquering Romans carried it into new territories around the Mediterranean. In 50 B.C., according to the Greek historian and geographer, Strabo, citizens of Corsica and Sardinia were praying to their gods for relief from the rabbits that fed on their crops. Norman invaders of the British Isles sent home for rabbits to provide a source of food for their people. Centuries later, Englishmen were cursing them with increasing fervor, as rabbit damage to agricultural crops increased to as much as 50,000,000 pounds sterling a year.

In spite of this, Englishmen taking up residence in foreign countries could not resist the urge to surround themselves in their new lands with rabbits from home. If Thomas Austin, however, could have peered into the future to hear what later generations of his Australian fellow citizens would say of him, he would perhaps have resisted his impulse.

In 1859 Austin ordered a dozen pairs of European rabbits from England. They arrived in fine condition on the good ship *Lightning* and were soon turned out to shift for themselves on Austin's estate in Victoria province. So nobly did the rabbits meet this new biological challenge that six years later Austin had killed a total of 20,000 rabbits on his ranch. And he estimated that he still had 10,000 remaining.

Down in New Zealand, meanwhile, some people looked with envy at Austin's triumph. They had tried, without success, for nearly three decades to establish European rabbits. Later New Zealand tried again, and this time, unfortunately, met with success.

When Thomas Austin's rabbits reached the borders of his Australian estate, they moved right on, and within a decade Australian officials and farmers were beginning to wonder if they had a monstrous problem on their hands. The answer came quickly enough. The rabbits were on the march.

Where the rabbits were now abundant, livestock had a difficult time finding enough to eat. Five rabbits, it was learned, ate as much as one ewe. Farmers shortly found their fields supporting fewer sheep than they ever had before. Landowners were forced into the rabbit business. One ranch in the Otago section of New Zealand supported 20,000 well-fed sheep until the first rabbit came on the scene. Within four years the flocks were reduced to 2000 sheep.

Australia became the world's largest source of rabbit meat. It also became the major supplier of felt, as rabbit furs went out by the shipload to the world market. In a single decade recently Australia shipped 157,000,000 frozen rabbits. In twenty-five years following 1873, New Zealand exported more than 200,000,000 rabbits to foreign ports. But rabbits proved a poor trade for sheep. The Australian and New Zealand economy suffered losses so large they could not be safely calculated.

The rabbits, however, did not march forward unchallenged. They were attacked with every weapon the Australians and New Zealanders could muster. In 1887, in New South Wales alone, they killed nearly 20,000,000 rabbits. Rabbit-proof fences were devised and in 1901 Australia began a rabbit-fencing project which would eventually stretch more than 2000 miles of wire, with the bottom buried in the ground and the top reinforced with added strands of barbed wire. Crossings and bridges were equipped with rabbit-proof gates. The cost of this fencing was $1,130,000 and it was still not a 100 per cent guarantee against the advancing rabbits.

The great attack of European rabbits on the Australian continent continued like a scourge for ninety years. People forgot the blessed days when the land was free of rabbits. Hundreds of millions of dollars had gone into fighting them. Men had won occasional battles but were still losing the war. Then the contest took a new and dramatic turn in 1950.

On the other side of the world, Brazilian cottontails were found in 1897 to carry a virus disease to which they apparently had a strong natural immunity. South American scientists had noticed, however, that domestic rabbits from European stock were not immune to the disease. In fact, wherever the virus attacked the domestic rabbits, the rabbits sickened and few recovered. The South American researchers speculated that this disease, caused by *Myxomatosis cuniculi*, might be an answer to the rabbit over-population in Australia and New Zealand.

In their laboratories the Australian scientists inoculated captive rabbits with the imported virus. The rabbits died. They then infected other animals and learned that the myxomatosis virus attacked neither the native marsupials nor humans.

Now they inoculated test rabbits with the deadly virus and turned them out like Typhoid Marys among the wild rabbits of New South Wales. But this diabolical plot against the rabbits seemed to be failing. In the following weeks scientists could find no trace of the disease in the wild rabbits. It was apparently one thing to infect rabbits by hand in the laboratories, quite another to have the forces of Nature take care of the chore outdoors. Once more the Australian scientists were ready to start looking elsewhere for the answer to their age-old rabbit troubles. But when summer came on, rabbits began dropping dead all over the countryside. The disease leaped forward along the stream valleys at more than twenty miles a week, leaving hundreds of thousands of dead rabbits in its wake.

Not since the end of World War II had there been such news in Australia. Word flashed to New Zealand and other parts of the world, wherever transplanted rabbits were an economic problem. New hopes were raised. From the open sores on sick rabbits the mosquitoes and flies continued to pick up the virus. And each time they bit a healthy rabbit they spread the disease. Autumn's cold killed the insects and halted the spread of myxomatosis.

But the following spring the Australian biologists again inoculated dozens of rabbits with the virus and then turned them loose in fields over much of the country. That summer of 1951–52 was a black one for the rabbits of Australia. The wildly raging epizootic swept them down in great numbers. The rabbits were lucky if five out of a thousand escaped. Those that did survive the virus still had to run a gauntlet of foxes, guns, and poisons.

Where the rabbits were being reduced, the fields soon began to show new signs of green vegetation, and "desert lands" once more became grazing lands. Livestock began to take over again from the rabbits.

If Australian farmers were convinced that their rabbit troubles were drawing to an end, the biologists were less certain. Biologist Walter E. Howard of the University of California spent a year as a Rhodes scholar working on the rabbit problem in New Zealand. Said Howard in 1959, "The virus is probably only a temporary relief in the countries where it has taken hold, because the virulence of the virus becomes lessened and rabbits develop immunity."

Meanwhile, however, the virus had practically eliminated rabbits in the British Isles, as well as France.

New Zealand had not shared the sudden dramatic success

of the Australians in the use of the virus. They lacked the insects to act as agents in spreading myxomatosis. Over the years New Zealanders used every method they could devise to kill rabbits. Rabbits were chased with dogs and ferrets. They were clubbed, shot, and trapped. Burrows were dug out or exposed to carbon bisulphide or cyanogen. Local people sometimes staged great circle drives which killed as many as 5000 rabbits before the pests could escape into their burrows. Where bridges crossed streams, they were equipped with special rabbit-proof gates because the rabbits apparently dislike swimming. Rabbit fences, however, were never as popular in New Zealand as they were in Australia.

Of all the methods used in New Zealand, the spreading of poison baits has probably been the most effective. Apples, carrots, jam, molasses, oats, and bran have been coated with strychnine, phosphorous, and arsenic and spread by the hundreds of tons across New Zealand fields. One locality used an airplane to spread 400 tons of poisoned carrots in a single season. Specialists devised a machine mounted on a truck chassis like a cement mixer to cut carrots and mix them with poison while they were hauled to the fields. The most devastating poison of all is 1080, a white powder of sodium fluoroacetate which came into widespread use by the U. S. Fish and Wildlife Service in its coyote-control work in western states. There is no antidote known for this controversial poison. In New Zealand 1080 was coated on baits which were spread in open furrows. After the rabbits had time to consume the deadly poison, the furrows were plowed in again to protect livestock which meanwhile had been removed from the treated fields.

Then New Zealand biologists began to notice that tall grass is a defense against rabbits. They favor short vegetation. And while it would seem that rabbits might crop it down themselves, it does not work out this way. Here was another land-management idea to be used in the long fight with the rabbits. After more than a century, neither Australia nor

New Zealand is yet free of its rabbits nor convinced it has found a final answer.

New Zealand's bill for rabbit-control work, according to Dr. Kazimierz A. Wodzicki, amounts to more than $4,000,-000 per year. Faced with such abundant evidence, men everywhere should see the trouble they court if they help the European rabbit spread to parts of the world spared its occupation to date. Even if the idea worked, having rabbits to hunt or run before the beagles seems scarcely enough excuse.

Chapter 21

The Unforgettable Quail

NORTH America's cherished bobwhite quail has an Old World cousin known as the coturnix who has absolutely refused, so far at least, to accept the multitude of invitations to come here and live. The coturnix is not so big as the bobwhite; in fact he is about two-thirds the size, and there are some other obvious differences you would see immediately if you were to look at the two side by side.

The coturnix appears to have a shorter tail in proportion to his size and looks almost bobtailed. Instead of a blunt seed-eater's beak like the bobwhite's, the coturnix has a longer beak, thinner and more pointed. The coturnix, also known as the stubble quail, seems to stick closer to the ground and even squats and crouches when feeding or walking about.

The coturnix gives a much different performance in flight from the bobwhite's. The bobwhite bounces from the ground with a startling thunderous take-off, flies rapidly, then glides before coming to earth. The coturnix rises rather quietly from a low angle, sometimes to the accompaniment of his own soft squeaking music, and keeps flailing away with whirring wings from the time he rises until the time he settles, which may be after covering a quarter of a mile. Perhaps you have seen a sora rail rise out of the cattails and depart; the coturnix gets away in much the same manner.

Unlike the bobwhite, coturnix do not covey up for the

night. When a group of them is scattered during the day by a gunner or dog, they depart in every direction, depending apparently on which way they are pointed at the moment.

The coturnix is feathered in a varied pattern of chocolate, browns, and lighter hues that change with the molts and differ between the sexes. It is also a highly productive bird. While the egg of the bobwhite must be incubated for twenty-three days, the coturnix chick hatches in sixteen. Bobwhites never nest until the year following their birth, but the coturnix female may be laying eggs and raising another brood while she is still wearing her juvenile plumage. It is common for coturnix hens to raise two broods of young in a year, with an average of ten chicks per brood, and some have been known to produce as many as four broods. The young are fully mature at fifty-one days of age, and in Missouri experiments coturnix only thirty-six days old produced fertile eggs.

It is understandable that outdoorsmen, knowing of this natural potential and of the bird's reputation for holding well before the bird dog, would be quick to dream of establishing coturnix quail in hope of providing more hunting.

What is the native home of this highly productive little quail? Historically, this is the migratory quail of Africa, Europe, and Asia. This is the quail mentioned in the Bible. It fed the Israelites as they came out of Egypt. There are the Japanese coturnix and the European coturnix, both of the same genus and much alike. In all of the birds in the order *Galliformes*, only the coturnix are highly migratory species. The European race migrates across the Mediterranean to Africa; the other branch of the family, which breeds in the Japanese islands, eastern Siberia, and North China, winters in southern China, Formosa, and other parts of South Asia. As it turned out, this migratory tendency would prove to be a major block in the plans of the coturnix-quail movers.

During 1875, large numbers of coturnix quail were

brought across the Atlantic from Italy and Sicily to the United States. They were transported to Ontario, Quebec, Maine, New Hampshire, Vermont, Massachusetts, New York, New Jersey, Pennsylvania, Ohio, and Virginia. The coturnix fever at the time was called an "absolute craze." In all of these places the little quail which seemed to hold such promise disappeared.

Then on June 8, 1880, 200 were released in Vermont. The cost was three dollars each. Hope still ran high and on May 5, 1880, another 5100 coturnix quail arrived from overseas and were released in sixteen different locations. Some were promptly taken by predators, some were seen around the points of release for a few weeks, and a few even nested that first year. Then autumn came and brought with it whatever triggers the inherent instinct for migration in the coturnix; the birds departed. A few were taken by hunters that fall as far south as Georgia and North Carolina. According to J. C. Phillips, recording the known facts about that introduction for the U. S. Department of Agriculture in 1928, ". . . after the migration there was never any return movement."

Reports told of exhausted coturnix landing on a ship several hundred miles southeast of Cape Hatteras, ". . . and the theory was prevalent at the time," Phillips said, "that most of the introduced birds migrated in a southeasterly direction and perished at sea."

Momentarily, the coturnix craze subsided and there seems to have been no more immediate introductions after 1881. Next the fever revived on the West Coast in 1904, when some Japanese coturnix were turned out in the state of Washington. That state came back for one more coturnix effort in 1923, when it turned out 500 coturnix from northern China. "As might have been expected from earlier experiences with practically the same species in the East," said Phillips, "the bird never took hold and soon disappeared."

One interesting sidelight of the coturnix craze of that

period, however, was that hundreds of the birds were being shipped from the Orient to Chinese restaurants in California. Eventually the state decided that the coturnix were "quail" and thus came under state regulations as game birds and consequently could not be marketed. California then seized thousands of the imported coturnix and either destroyed or released them. The last big shipment reached port in 1904. In the four previous years 19,000 coturnix quail had been brought into the state for the restaurant trade.

Gradually the urge to bring more of these little quail into the country quieted and lay dormant. But the idea was far from dead, as the events of 1956 proved. That year Missouri's Conservation Commission once again set the coturnix bandwagon in full motion.

The chain of events had actually begun a few years earlier after two Missouri biologists observed the exotic coturnix while studying birds in Hawaii. They later reported their findings on the birds' habitat and food requirements in an unpublished paper called "A consideration of the common quail (*Coturnix coturnix*) of the Old World for possible introduction in Missouri."

Melvin O. Steen, director of the Missouri Fish and Game Commission, discussed the idea at meetings of the International Association of Game and Fish Commissioners.

State fish and game departments, it should be understood, are often hard-pressed to increase the supplies of game and fish, whether it can be done or not. In this atmosphere it is easy to continue such discredited wildlife-management practices as artificial stocking, winter feeding, and predator control, or yield to the temptation to import foreign species that might help quiet public demands.

Having made the fateful decision that the coturnix quail was worthy of another gamble, Mel Steen appointed Jack A. Stanford, a well-qualified wildlife biologist, to head up a carefully planned coturnix research program.

Missouri's wildlife specialists agreed that the former efforts with coturnix had been poorly planned, poorly managed, and that the birds had been turned out in numbers too small to give them a good chance of success. They intended to correct all three of these faults. But there was no way of telling with certainty where, if anywhere, the birds might have the best chance without actually trying them in the field. Hopefully, if they were widely released, in substantial numbers, they might somewhere fall into suitable habitat, then spread out from that locus.

Missouri soon had a host of other state game and fish departments chasing the coturnix rainbow. In some of these, it should be noted, the wildlife biologists approached the idea with considerably less enthusiasm than did their bosses. "Our director," said the chief game biologist of one midwestern state, "just told us he had bought some and we were to try them. Period." The plan had begun in the individual states and was proceeding without any co-ordination or official enthusiasm from federal workers in the Fish and Wildlife Service. As might have been expected, coturnix projects were not handled in a uniform manner from state to state.

Tempering the enthusiasm generated by the coturnix advocates, however, were the solemn warnings of wildlife authorities who saw nothing but trouble and waste in the idea. From Dr. Clarence Cottam, director of the Welder Wildlife Foundation in Texas, came the opinion that ". . . a migrant bird likely will not succeed in the United States." He pointed out the history of past introductions of coturnix and flatly predicted a costly failure. In spite of these predictions and similar ones from some other concerned ecologists, the coturnix fever mounted.

Stanford and a few others were concerned about the willingness of some states to play the coturnix tune for its full publicity value while ignoring the need for serious biological analysis of the bird's reaction to its new habitat. It seemed a completely natural procedure for each state purchasing its first stock of coturnix quail to announce the bird's arrival through its regular weekly news releases. In New Hampshire (where coturnix had been unsuccessfully released in 1875) a news story in 1957 announced that the Fish and Game Department had purchased ten pairs of coturnix. "If observations and tests indicate that the coturnix can be successfully established in the Granite State," said the release, "it is felt that they will serve as a buffer species, furnish more targets for the sportsmen, and be an economical means of producing additional bird hunting."

Several states, however, promptly went much further than this type of calm announcement. Some quickly invited sportsmen's clubs to participate in the project. Some offered to give coturnix quail to clubs for release. One state announced to its game protectors and public relations workers that the coturnix was now available for their use in talks before clubs and on television.

Before long the publicity had snowballed. Outdoorsmen everywhere had a new word in their vocabulary. This exciting new game bird promised to be nothing short of fantastic. And many people asked why no one had thought of this miraculous bird sooner. "In this widespread activity," Jack Stanford said in a 1957 talk before a group of his fellow biologists from several states, "the known and unknown biological characteristics of the birds have been so exaggerated and glorified that sportsmen of all descriptions have joined to release additional hundreds of banded and unbanded quail and to help gather information on 'our new' game bird. . . . The whole misconception started through poorly presented facts. Undoubtedly some misleading information was public relations fodder to let the hunting license buyer and the pressure groups know that the old department was really going to town with something red-hot for them."

Biologically, one unanswered riddle haunting wildlife specialists was the possible relationship of the coturnix to the native bobwhite—which everyone agreed from the beginning was a superior and more desirable bird in every way than the Old World quail could hope to become. The new import had been widely billed as the "stubble quail." The idea spread that stubble fields were wildlife wastelands. Coturnix promoters were saying, as Stanford pointed out, that ". . . we have it licked with coturnix as the birds will even go to town in stubble." He then added solemnly, however, that "in Missouri, stubble provides the finest bobwhite-quail habitat." Stanford, who probably understood the foreign bird as well as anyone in the country, added that ". . . the coturnix is a bird which appears to select habitat similar to that of bobwhite quail."

Missouri obtained 110 wild coturnix from Pakistan in 1955. After the birds were installed in holding pens in this country, free-running dogs broke in and destroyed them. Next came a shipment of birds from Hawaii, but these birds died in the express depot before they could be picked up. Then Missouri turned to an importer of foreign birds in California and made arrangements to buy seventy pairs of coturnix. These were from breeding stock imported from Japan in 1953. Missouri leased a hatchery, installed the coturnix, and was now launched on phase two of the plan. If the idea was to succeed, there was a need for large numbers of coturnix quail. From here on, the aim was mass production.

So well did the quail do at producing eggs, and so contented were they in captivity, that one might almost have wondered if Missouri had purchased domesticated, not wild, birds. This indeed was later given as one reason for the eventual outcome of the project. It is known that in Asia these birds are kept in little bamboo cages for commercial egg production. In rooms where light and temperature are under constant control, they are fed high-protein diets of fish and grains. Under such conditions they rival leghorn hens in egg production and lay from 150 to 250 eggs per year.

If it was a large stock of birds the experimenters wanted, they soon had the order filled by the co-operative coturnix.

Not only were there birds enough for Missouri's release plan but there were also plenty to sell brood stock to other eager states.

Within the following two or three years, coturnix quail were released, often by the thousands, in nineteen states and one Canadian province. Twelve states, including Florida, Illinois, Indiana, Kentucky, Missouri, Nebraska, New Hampshire, North Carolina, Ohio, Oklahoma, Tennessee, and Texas, agreed to exchange information on what they learned about the habits of the coturnix.

By July 1958, state game departments had released 363,-128 coturnix quail on American soil. In addition, four states had turned over 19,000 eggs and 60,000 young birds to sportsmen for propagation and release. Meanwhile, commercial game farms and hatcherymen had climbed aboard the coturnix band wagon, and in nearly two-thirds of the states individuals and clubs had purchased and released uncounted numbers of these coturnix. The total number of coturnix released in this country in that brief two-year period perhaps never will be accurately computed, but the minimum number established from the above figures is only a fraction of the total.

Thus it would seem that the bird had been given a fair chance. Judge Owen Denny, it could be recalled, had started all the pheasants in Oregon, and several other states as well, with his shipment of twenty-eight ringnecks released in suitable habitat.

From 1955 through 1958, Missouri, which released 35,-000 coturnix within its borders, spent $94,507.97 on the project. Many states never released cost figures. Most of the states received federal aid to help finance their coturnix studies under the Pittman-Robertson program.

What happened when these birds were turned out? The results were similar in most states and Indiana's story is perhaps typical.

In April 1956 Indiana wildlife biologists in the Department

of Conservation found themselves with fifty pairs of coturnix in their care. The birds had been purchased from Missouri at a cost of $600, or six dollars each. From this modest beginning, coturnix were shortly coming from the Muscatatuck Game Farm near North Vernon, Indiana, by the hundreds. During the next three seasons the state's wildlife technicians released 28,052 of the birds into various parts of Indiana. Meanwhile, hopeful sportsmen noticed that various commercial game farms advertised coturnix quail in the outdoor magazines, so they purchased and released at least 1281 of the birds in their eagerness to "do something."

Several phases of the project were under way simultaneously. While hatchery personnel were learning how to turn out scores of coturnix, wildlife biologists were busily studying soil maps, climatic conditions, and agricultural practices in the effort to select suitable release sites. They chose four regions of the state for the critical tests.

One was in the heavily farmed, fertile, flat farmlands of Grant County near Fairmount. Another was in Montgomery County, where fields are large, fence rows clean, and farming highly mechanized. A third was in the submarginal sandy country of Newton County, on the Willow Slough State Fish and Game Area. And the fourth location was that region of potholes, marshes, lakes, and scattered and varied farming in a part of Kosciusko County once covered by an ancient lake. These locations, centered in the northern part of the state, gave the new birds room for southern migration before sighting the Ohio River and leaving the state which was befriending them.

The fate of the birds once released was in the hands of the gods, and their future was uniformly bleak and short-lived. What happened to 2019 coturnix given their freedom on the Grant County area, April 17, 1957, was similar in many ways to what happened to all the coturnix released in Indiana during this study period. For that matter, it was a drama being repeated in numerous states across the country about the same time.

The project leader assembled with his crew and his crates of chattering coturnix in an ungrazed woodlot bordering a fifteen-acre alfalfa field. The crew first spread 100 pounds of cracked corn near the release sight, then turned the birds out where it was do or die. According to the official report of the day's activities, "The released birds immediately began mating, eating corn and insects, dusting and flying."

By evening the 2000 coturnix quail had spread over at least eight acres of woods and alfalfa, and a minimum of eight were found dead. The observers noticed a disturbing tendency of the weak-flying birds to dash themselves into woven wire fences and the branches of trees.

A few of the birds had drowned during a heavy rainstorm the first night. One had been decapitated. A farm dog was seen to catch three whose bodies were subsequently eaten by crows. One coturnix was seen eating violet leaves while a second one was observed feeding on the leaves of spring beauties. But a minimum of 200 were huddled within fifteen feet of the cracked corn.

On April 19, twenty-one dead coturnix were found in the woods, eight of them judged to be the victims of avian predators. That afternoon a Cooper's hawk was noticed loafing around the woods. Meanwhile, the coturnix were still knocking themselves out on fences and branches.

On April 21 two dead coturnix were found by a stump, three more in the woodlot, seven in the alfalfa field. A farmer living a short distance to the southeast delivered to the project leader bands of four birds carried home by his cats, while the farmer's tenant came around with bands of two more birds caught by his cats. Other coturnix continued to add their band numbers to the rolls of the deceased through the following weeks, and farmers as far as three and four miles away occasionally reported seeing or hearing some of the birds.

Two months after the initial release the wildlife technicians turned out a second planting of 2031 six- to eight-week old coturnix a few miles to the north of the first site and began their intensive watch.

During the following weeks various hawks moved into the area and coturnix leg bands were found beneath the trees where the hawks fed. As the coturnix spread toward outlying farmsteads, domestic cats greeted them. The wildlife specialists attributed these heavy losses to predators suddenly confronted with new and easily caught prey. Some successful nesting of coturnix was known to have occurred.

By the second week in November, however, coturnix were no longer seen on the study area. Later in the month at least two of the birds were killed elsewhere in Indiana. Apparently the migration urge was driving the coturnix out of the release area. Eventually, when all the reports were tallied, twenty-seven bands were recovered from outside the counties where the birds were freed. Bands had been mailed back from nine states, including Maryland, Virginia, Alabama, and Mississippi. The longest any of these birds had lived in the wild was six months. The birds had moved in every direction, but mostly south and southeast until, it is believed, they left the continent and tried, in vain, to cross the ocean.

By 1958 there was widespread conviction even among those who had held the greatest hope for these little birds that the plan was destined for failure. The three-year project was now completed, and in state after state the coturnix experiment ended as suddenly as it had begun. Some felt that a different strain of coturnix quail might have had a better chance, and it may be that we have not yet heard the last of the "stubble" quail.

Because the coturnix has consistently failed, we still do not know how it might have measured up as an addition to the American fauna. We have no assurance that it would not compete seriously with the bobwhite or become an agricultural plague. It has the reproductive potential of the starling or the house sparrow. And in what manner its feeding habits might change if it lived in western wheat fields or southern soybean fields is speculative.

Not everyone was sorry to see this latest demise of the coturnix. One midwestern state biologist forced into the program by his chief administrator said later that "when it caved in, we all heaved a sigh of relief." Elsewhere, biologists and ecologists who had warned against the costly and hazardous plan from the beginning labeled it what it had now become —"a miserable failure."

This then is the most recent chapter in the saga of the coturnix quail, which is probably destined to be paraded out again at some future time as the promising new miracle bird and an answer to an alleged shortage of native game birds.

WILDLIFE ROULETTE

Chapter 22

Still Chasing Rainbows

———— ⚘ ————

PURSUIT of strange foreign creatures has been a perpetual race, a relay, with one generation passing the stick to the next. At the slightest promise of an elusive exotic prize, we're off and running, butterfly net at the ready, enthusiasm undampened by past mistakes.

With all the wild species scattered to the corners of the earth, the mathematical possibilities for new combinations in any area are staggering. And even when we have tried them all, we will not be finished, because most of them will fail and we will have to go back and try them again and again.

Wildlife movers appear as busy today as ever. Now, a century and more since the full flowering of the acclimatization societies, we have changed our approach somewhat but we have not given up. Individuals and little bands of private citizens still engage in the introduction of new wildlife species. But today the government has become the biggest acclimatization society of all. Both state and federal governments search out and import foreign wildlife. The motivations for this animal moving have undergone some shifting in emphasis. Sentiment and homesickness no longer play the role they did during the nineteenth century.

Modern-day interest in importing exotic wildlife centers in the state capitals. "We will probably go right on bringing in foreign species," says one noted ecologist, "as long as the state fish and game administrators see it as a cure-all for wildlife shortages." To understand the atmosphere that fosters the continuation of this costly and usually futile effort, we should look briefly at the arrangement of a typical state game and fish department.

The director of the department may be either a career wildlife administrator, a temporarily employed political appointee, or both, depending on the state in which he works. In most states there is a fish and game commission to which he supposedly answers. Commission members hold appointments from the governor, often granted as political favors or prestige awards without serious consideration of the appointee's qualifications.

Then there is the state legislature casting its shadow over the lot of them, clerks, wardens, biologists, administrators, and commissioners. And it is the rare and valued state legislator who either knows or cares much about wildlife technology or the realities of managing our valuable natural resources. Consequently, biological science all too often is at the mercy of practical politics.

This puts the ultimate power of resource management in the hands of the voting citizen, who is too often prone to assume that he is striking a blow for conservation simply by demanding that we "do something to get better hunting and fishing." In this atmosphere it is the rare fish and game department chief who believes that new wildlife species should not be tried. Nor is he willing to give up without a fight his "state's rights" to a higher authority that might prohibit or control such importations in the future.

World War II might have been a factor in introducing traveling Americans to some of the great variety of game birds in other parts of the world. A few wildlife biologists in the armed forces predicted that returning servicemen would bring mounting pressure on state game and fish departments for the introduction of these foreign species.

The topic was discussed in the Fish and Wildlife Service and among members of the International Association of

Game and Fish Commissioners. Some pointed out that there was nothing to keep those who cared to do so from bringing in new species of game birds and releasing them. This conclusion became the springboard for a plan to bring all the groups together in one program—not for the laudable purpose of discouraging importation of foreign game birds—but to seek out likely candidates and facilitate their introduction to those states requesting them. The leading advocate and moving force in this plan was Dr. Gardiner Bump, wildlife biologist and an ex-army officer. Once the Foreign Game Program was established, Dr. Bump was appointed by the Fish and Wildlife Service as the biologist in charge of it. Now the federal government was formally in the exotic-animal business.

Speaking before his fellow professionals at the sixteenth North American Wildlife Conference in 1951, Dr. Bump admitted that the importation of exotics is a hazardous business and that it has usually been a big waste of money. These, he felt, were reasons calling for a serious, well-planned approach.

Why—in the face of repeated failures—should the efforts continue? Here the proponents always find the reason in the shortsightedness of earlier animal movers. As Dr. Bump explained it, "Few have been carefully planned; none scientifically carried out." The answer then, it would appear, is simply to apply the scientific techniques we might have mastered over the years, plus principles of sound planning.

Dr. Bump's preliminary studies showed that, until 1940, we had released twenty-nine species of game birds, plus forty-four species of other birds in the United States. He pointed out that these were on a "hit-or-miss" basis, some considered fortunate, most highly unfortunate. Work began on two fronts. While Dr. Bump headed for Asia to observe the game birds abundant there, co-operating state biologists were urged to map their "game-deficient" areas. By 1963, when speaking before the twenty-eighth North American Wildlife and Natural Resources Conference, Dr. Bump would be able to say, "Co-operative agreements with forty-five of the fifty states have been signed. Most of these states, at our request, have prepared written ecological descriptions and appraisals of their problem habitats as a basis for determining the character and extent of the areas they consider to be game-deficient." The "problem areas" considered lacking in suitable game birds covered a fifth of the United States and were in all parts of the country.

In his program's first fifteen years, Dr. Bump traveled over Asia and Europe and made ecological studies of more than 100 game-bird species. One out of five gained the government stamp of approval for trial release or game-farm propagation back in the United States. Correspondence, meanwhile, flowed steadily between Dr. Bump and numerous state wildlife agencies. From letters, and sometimes photographs, the state-side biologists attempted to choose habitat outwardly similar in climate and vegetation to what the test birds occupied in their native lands. Among these birds were partridges, pheasants, sand grouse, and jungle fowl. The migratory coturnix quail, incidentally, was never recommended by Dr. Bump. There is nothing to keep state administrators who are discontented with the speed or results of the federal program from striking boldly off on their own—precisely what they did with the coturnix.

While Dr. Bump's aim was to make the program scientific in approach, there were on the sidelines respected scientists convinced that we did not know enough to make it truly scientific, and that the ecological studies of birds in their native lands were inadequate.

From Dr. Bump's list of wild candidates for American citizenship, state wildlife workers began to pick and choose the birds they would offer their game commissions. Once everyone agreed, the state was to arrange for transportation, quarantine, and care of the birds. The Wildlife Management Institute, acting as an agent between state and federal government, paid transportation costs and later billed the state for the amount spent. The states, meanwhile, must agree to continue the programs for at least three years to give the new birds a chance.

Such programs are federally subsidized under the Pittman-Robertson program. This means that the game importations are paid for three-fourths by the federal government, one-fourth by the state. Pittman-Robertson funds, it should be understood, are collected from a tax of eleven per cent that sportsmen pay on arms and ammunition. The money is pro-rated back to the states for wildlife research management, and land acquisition.

One of the foreign birds that Dr. Bump first considered was Europe's giant grouse, the capercaillie. Earlier Americans had also cast longing glances at this impressive bird. In 1893 a pair was shipped to Rhode Island. Two years later another small shipment went to Maine. Then, between 1904 and 1907, a total of 471 were released in the forests of Michigan, the Adirondacks, and British Columbia. They displayed marked inability to adapt to these new conditions. The experiment failed.

The shipment Dr. Bump sent to Wisconsin at that state's request totaled twenty-six birds. With them were five black grouse, all live-trapped in the Scandinavian countries. While concerned naturalists worried about the competition these foreigners might offer native grouse if they should become established, evidence accumulated that some unhealthy birds had slipped by the U. S. Department of Agriculture's Bureau of Animal Quarantine. Some died before they could be turned out in the Wisconsin woods. Technicians made microscopic examinations of their blood and discovered internal parasites. The birds that were released, however, did not adjust to Wisconsin living and disappeared within two years.

Next on the list were 3000 Turkish chukar partridges divided among three states for release over a four-year period. Nevada then released 1400 common Indian sand grouse wild-trapped in the Thar Desert in India. They disappeared. A year and a half after their release two of the birds were shot flying together near Navojoa, Sonora, Mexico. The biologists never knew how many of the sand grouse had crossed the international border. Nor does anyone know whether or not they could become a destructive pest in the small grain and rice fields of the irrigated valleys. The sand grouse has been quietly withdrawn from the list of candidates—at least in Nevada.

Other birds imported included pheasants that might survive in the Southeast where the ringneck cannot prosper. In 1963, twenty-three states and Guam were carrying out test releases of sixteen species of game birds plus five additional cross-bred strains of pheasants. And in the preceding three years Dr. Bump had shipped to his co-operating states 16,145 live-trapped foreign game birds for propagation and release.

Meanwhile, the endless search extended to South America, with government biologists sifting through the world's list of 1000 species and sub-species of game birds, hoping that somewhere, somehow, they might, with their modern approach, emulate the good luck Judge Owen N. Denny had with the ringneck pheasant back in 1881.

Out in the wet world of the fishes this old game of musical chairs for wildlife was being played with equal enthusiasm. The fish rearrangers seem busier today than ever before. Fish of wide variety from greatly separated parts of the world are being endlessly reshuffled.

Recent releases from state fish and game departments tell of the many species being brought in from outside the country, and others being moved to new sections of the United States where they did not previously live. Arkansas recently completed a trade in which it sent some of its channel catfish to Florida in exchange for 32,000 fry of the Florida large-mouth bass. Ohio's Division of Wildlife shipped 20,000 eyed eggs of the chain pickerel to French Morocco. Meanwhile, Michigan was working toward introduction of three new fish, kokanee and coho salmon and the anadromous striped bass, which some fear might compete with Michigan's excellent bass, walleyes, and lake trout. Nevada, meanwhile, was introducing the white bass, a fresh-water cousin of the striped bass, and was also turning out a shipment of channel catfish. And all these examples totaled but a small fraction of the fish transplanting under way in recent years.

In 1938 and 1939, fish culturists in Java began pond-rearing of a mouthbreeder, a member of the big family of cichlids with the formal name of *Tilapia mossambica*. The fish, called "tilapia" for short, has in recent times spread far beyond its native range. The female tilapia produces 100 to 300 young at a time, depending on her size, and in tropical waters can bring off a new brood every thirty to forty days. She carries the incubating eggs in her mouth. In some species the male carries them. The adults may reach weights up to five pounds. They feed upon a wide variety of plant and animal matter.

The poundage of tilapia that a one-acre pond can produce is sometimes a wonder to behold. Word was soon spreading that this fish, with no attention at all, averaged an annual protein production of 292 pounds per acre. But that was a drop in the fish pond compared with the true potential of the fish. With fertilization and feeding, according to a report from Taiwan, tilapia could annually produce six to eight tons of protein per acre. Meanwhile, in sewage ponds in Indonesia, it was found to produce 5600 pounds per acre. What else did a fish have to do to attract wide attention in a hungry world? Throughout Asia it was welcomed as a wonder fish. Japanese fish culturists transferred it, during World War II, to occupied Thailand, Burma, Sumatra, and Malacca. Soon it was on its way to the Philippines, Formosa, Ceylon, Malaya, British West Indies, Puerto Rico, India, Trinidad, Pakistan, Borneo, Hawaii, and the United States mainland.

Unlike many other foreign species introduced into the United States before and since, this one was first tested by a meticulous and highly qualified biologist. The shipment reached Auburn, Alabama, in 1954 where it was delivered to Professor H. S. Swingle of the Alabama Polytechnic Institute. The first step Dr. Swingle took was to disinfect the newly arrived tilapia. Then he isolated them in aquaria for three to five months, examining them frequently for evidence of parasites or disease. He knew that this tropical species had definite temperature limitations. Tests in a cold room showed that the tilapia ceased breeding when water temperatures dropped below sixty degrees Fahrenheit, and died at forty-eight degrees. This clearly meant that there was no chance of their winter survival anywhere north of Central Florida.

As a summer resident of Alabama ponds, tilapia, Dr. Swingle found, out-produced bluegills by three times the weight and fed heavily on the troublesome algae. But the fish had to be taken indoors for the winter. This reduced the length of time each year they could be caught by sport fishermen because a growing period had to be allowed following the time they were turned out again in the spring.

In some places where the tilapia were introduced, this very ability to reproduce rapidly had brought it into some disfavor. Ponds filled up with stunted fish too small to eat. And because this species can also live in salt water it was found in the Philippines to compete with the milkfish, which is more highly valued.

What would happen if tilapia were to become stocked in waters of Central Florida and southward where it might live the year round? The Florida Game and Fresh Water Fish Commission decided in 1961 to find out the quick way. Three thousand fingerlings, brought in from Alabama, were released in a pond in the Tampa Bay area.

There seems little chance this fish will become a valuable addition to Florida's rich inheritance of native fishes. The tilapia was soon proving that unless kept under control it spawns at a very small size and fills ponds with stunted fish that are unattractive to anglers. And to keep them under control would call for a harvest of perhaps ninety per cent each year. This would be a virtual impossibility for anglers to accomplish, even if the fish were large enough to appeal to them. The only control method known to remain is poison and in lakes with mixed fish populations this is not practical because tilapia, as was learned in Alabama previously, are considerably more resistant to rotenone poisoning than are the native game fish, and poisoning heavily enough to kill tilapia would kill the desirable fish first.

Another answer to the tilapia's staggering productivity and its ability to overcrowd quickly a pond with stunted fish came as a by-product of research done for another purpose by biologists in Malaya who had crossbred two races of tilapia, males from the island of Zanzibar and females from East Africa. Two of the results of the crossbreeding were that the offspring were bigger than either parent and that they were all males. Biologists in Arizona obtained the two races, crossbred them, and turned them out in ponds near Tucson. Here was a tilapia that men could keep under control, providing only the hybrids were set free.

Another reason tilapia transplants into Florida have fisheries biologists worried is that there are about 600 species of cichlids for the experimenters to draw from. "My concern," says Dr. C. Richard Robins, professor of marine science at the world-famous Institute of Marine Science in Miami, Florida, "is that most species of *Tilapia* are very difficult to distinguish and each has its own habits and tolerances. If the introduction of *Tilapia* is undertaken on a large scale, then untested species will probably enter our waters."

But the tilapia is not the only foreign fish with which Florida has recently polluted its native fauna. The state recently and purposely introduced large numbers of another cichlid, Tucunare, a native of South America and a possible competitor of Florida's famed largemouth bass, the fish that annually lures millions of dollars of out-of-state tourist business. Fisheries biologists outside the Florida Game and Fresh Water Fish Commission look upon this as another fish introduced far too casually. And even its sport-fishing qualities are questionable.

Meanwhile, in the Miami area there is still another strange fish. Tropical-fish hobbyists have dumped hundreds of them out in the local waters to get rid of them. This is the fish known in scientific circles as *Astronotus ocellatus*, a South American native that reproduces every three weeks. This one does have some sport-fishing attributes, although, as one experienced Florida fisherman concludes, "Nobody would class it with the snook or the bass." There is, of course, always the threat that it will suddenly reach a level in numbers potentially dangerous to Florida's other fish.

It is still perfectly legal to import the man-eating piranha into the United States by permit, and thousands of them do come in every year for the hobby trade. The Secretary of the Interior has been reluctant to prohibit their importation because such an order would distress the tropical-fish business. There are some thirty species that can be easily confused with the four that will attack warm-blooded prey, including man. To be perfectly safe they would all have to be prohibited.

Some authorities doubt that the piranha could live in the wild in the United States, even in southern Florida. And the chance they might reproduce and establish prospering populations seems even less likely. But biologists also know that the limits of tolerance of a living organism may alter under new environmental conditions. There is always the lurking probability that this could happen in Florida and give that state one more doubtful claim to fame—the only wild population of piranha in North America. Dr. Robins, incidentally, is convinced that the piranha could become established in Florida waters.

Meanwhile, Texas ranchers turn out African big game, zoological gardens retain free-flying collections of birds, fishermen dump excess bait minnows into new waters, well-meaning sportsmen's clubs stock waters with new species of fish, and hobbyists bring in, and sometimes release, cage birds and exotic fishes. One fishing-tackle manufacturer even shipped 1200 alligator-like Central American caymans recently all over the country as premiums in a promotion campaign.

The human being is set apart from his fellow creatures by virtue of the ability to apply recorded knowledge. Supposedly, each new generation has more to guide it than did its parent generation. We may, however, be prone to overrate the difference between what we know and what Grandpa knew.

What is needed is an appreciation for the immensity of the unknown. Transferring the world's wildlife from one habitat, balanced or not balanced, to an entirely foreign habitat, balanced or not balanced, is a challenge no man can meet with guaranteed impunity.

Scientists who oppose wildlife introductions do so for numerous reasons—none of which are easily dismissed. One of these is the recognized fact that no one can safely predict how an animal will act under the stress of new ecological conditions. It may change its habits completely and there are many examples to prove it.

Who could have predicted that the American gray squirrel, once released in England, would change its food habits and become a bark eater?

The New Zealand parrot, *Nestor notabilis*, once restricted itself to a diet of carrion, vegetable matter, and insects. After white men changed the environment by introducing sheep, however, the parrot developed a fondness for that fat which lies around the kidney of a sheep. Eventually, to the surprise of everyone, including presumably the sheep, the parrot began feeding on the live sheep by digging into their backs to get the fat.

The biologist is always concerned with the effect of imported species on native wildlife. The average outdoorsman is too little aware of the great trouble these foreigners might visit on the natives. Any new organism established in a wild community alters the natural balance. The changes may be so slight most of us would never detect them. Or they may be so drastic that everyone can readily see them.

An unpredicted development occurred in the 1940s on the Japanese island of Oshima after some Formosan golden-backed squirrels escaped from a zoological garden. The squirrels prospered. Shortly an estimated 20,000 of them were running over the island. The squirrels chased the Japanese white-eyes, a yellowish, warbler-sized bird, away from the camellia blossoms. This was bad because the white-eyes, which have a fondness for nectar, cross-pollinate the flowers. The production of camellia oil, the island's major export commodity, fell drastically.

In Lake Atitlán, far up in the mountains of Guatemala, largemouth bass were introduced in 1956 with unexpected results. In this and other Central American countries bass have been moved into numerous new waters, and in some cases prospered so greatly that they provide commercial fishing. But the mile-high Lake Atitlán is the last domain of the nearly extinct giant pied-billed grebe, a species similar to the common pied-billed grebe, but about fifty per cent larger. Grebes are primitive birds that build floating nests, feed on fish, are not strong fliers, and are seldom far from water. The giant pied-billed grebe cannot fly at all.

When the bass came to Atitlán, there were an estimated 200 of the giant pied-billed grebes remaining. As the bass grew larger, the birds became increasingly rare. Biologists on the scene studying the tragedy placed the blame largely on the imported fish. The big bass are said to eat the young of the rare grebes as quickly as they hatch and leave the nest. And it is probably too late now to keep the imported bass from speeding the extinction of the giant pied-billed grebe.

Half a century earlier on a tiny, partly wooded island, between New Zealand's north and south islands, a similar and almost forgotten tragedy evolved. The keeper of the government lighthouse on Stephen Island was also the keeper of a cat, which one day came home bearing the carcass of a small wren. The cat's owner made the wren into a scientific mount and sent the skin to the famed British ornithologist, Lord Rothschild, who announced that the cat had discovered a previously unknown species. The bird became known as the Stephen's Island wren. The cat continued to bring in the wrens. The lighthouse keeper continued to mount the skins and ship them to London, but after about a dozen the supply ran out. The cat had attained the dubious honor of having brought to extinction, without help, a native species of bird that had perhaps never been seen alive by man. The skin of the first one is today in the reference collection of The American Museum of Natural History, halfway around the world from where the cat collected its rare prize.

When the Portuguese discovered the island of Mauritius, about 1507, the strange-looking dodo lived there. The sailors took the dodos to eat, in spite of the fact that they are said to have been exceedingly tough except for the breast. But perhaps even more important was the fact that hogs released on the island destroyed some of the dodo nests and were aided in the deed by imported monkeys, cats, and rats. These rare birds were gone from the island about 1680.

Native and foreign species sometimes compete directly for available food supplies. Burros in the deserts of the Southwest compete with the endangered desert bighorn sheep for both food and water. Rabbits when overpopulating an area compete with every local herbivorous animal, wild or domestic.

In 1891, at the dawn of the Gay Nineties, Dr. Sheldon Jackson, United States General Agent for Education in Alaska, decided that the native Eskimo people should have reindeer. It sounded logical. The people needed meat and another source of income. And out there was all that barren tundra, growing reindeer moss. The government began importing reindeer from Siberia, complete with Lapland herders.

The semi-domesticated reindeer increased during the following years, and by 1940 there were 252,500. But they were down to 155,000 in 1941 and by 1950 there were only 25,000 left.

Behind this drastic depletion of Alaska's imported reindeer herds was a complex mixture of economic, biological, and human factors which are still the subject of much argument. Some blamed the non-native businessmen which the government had permitted to dominate the industry. Others blamed the wolves, the Eskimos, the government policies, and the failing range. Some of the reindeer wandered off with migrating herds of caribou. The herds in some areas doubtless had exceeded the carrying capacity of the range. The lichens on which they feed sometimes require a quarter of a century or longer to replace their growth, and the grazing reindeer had introduced a whole new factor into the ecology of the Alaskan tundra. The Eskimos proved reluctant to forsake their home territories and give up their ancient way of life as hunters. Suddenly they had been asked to become wandering herdsmen.

When hopes were looking bright for reindeer in Alaska, Michigan authorities suddenly decided that they, too, would like some reindeer for stocking in the Upper Peninsula. Because the federal government wanted $600 a head for its precious Alaskan stock, Michigan turned directly to Norwegian sources and in 1922 imported sixty reindeer and two Lapland herders. Within five years all of the animals had inexplicably languished and passed away. The last of the Michigan reindeer to go was a sad-eyed old cow who spent her final days in the Belle Isle Zoo. The experiment cost $125,000.

Dr. Ward M. Sharp, working on the Valentine National Wildlife Refuge in the Nebraska sandhills between 1937 and 1942, described what happens when imported cock pheasants and the male prairie chickens conflict on the chicken's booming grounds. When the cock pheasant tried to chase a prairie chicken from the area, the prairie chicken would ". . . square off at a pheasant in typical rooster fashion," recorded Dr. Sharp. "After some sparring, the pheasant and prairie chicken would rush together and meet in mid-air. The pheasant was so much faster, inflicting punishment with its spurs, that the prairie chicken would take a very rough flogging before freeing himself from the situation. Being roundly defeated and pummeled, it would run and take to flight at its first opportunity. The cock pheasant would take chase, driving the prairie chicken for a distance. A cock pheasant," Dr. Sharp concluded, "may eventually drive all prairie chickens from a meadow or booming area during the spring breeding season."

He also notes that there was a decline in prairie chicken numbers in the Nebraska sandhills during the 1936–43 period when the pheasant numbers were climbing to new highs.

Biologists are also concerned over the possibility that introduced species might hybridize with closely related native forms and thus lead to the extinction of a species. Mallards introduced into New Zealand, for example, have crossbred with the native gray duck.

There is frequent conjecture that low population levels of bobwhite quail in northern states resulted from the release of less winter-hardy strains from the South. Two exotic species of wild goats were released in the High Tatra Mountains of Czechoslovakia. They mixed with the native wild goats, which had been reintroduced themselves, and all three interbred. The resulting breeding season, however, was so altered that the crossbred offspring came in midwinter and perished in the cold.

Professional wildlife workers sometimes advance a further objection to exotic species. Such projects drain off great sums of money from the management of the native wildlife. It is understandable that the wildlife specialists would consider native wildlife more desirable. In a sense, the importation of a foreign animal is an admission of defeat. The wildlife manager is a habitat manager.

Michigan's long-time conservation administrator and authority on the whitetail deer, Harry D. Ruhl, said before the fifth North American Wildlife Conference that "the value of introductions is far overestimated by the public and by too many game administrators. Where the choice exists," he added, "it is usually better to work with native rather than exotic species." Other authorities have repeatedly made similar observations. It may, however, be an oversimplification to assume that if money were not spent on exotics it would automatically be spent on management of native wildlife. Frequently it is easier to get appropriations for one more spectacular exotic animal scheme than for management of native species.

Research has brought new evidence in recent years that moving wildlife around the world presents serious health hazards. Pheasants are known to be carriers of infectious equine encephalomyelitis, or sleeping sickness in horses, and the virus causing the sickness is transmissible to man. One medical research specialist who long suspected the role of migrating birds in the spread of human diseases and death was Dr. Harry Hoogstraal. As head of a program in zoological research for the U. S. Naval Medical Research Unit in Cairo, Egypt, Dr. Hoogstraal noted that various tick-borne diseases were appearing in new and distant areas. He suspected that ticks carrying the viruses were hitchhiking across Europe and Asia on migrating birds. "Birds are already known," said Dr. Hoogstraal, "to be hosts of several viruses pathogenic to man and domestic animals, and the part they play in spreading such viruses is all the greater if they harbor ticks as well." By trapping various species of migrating birds, Dr. Hoogstraal was able to verify his deduction, and the results of his research were covered in the bulletin of the World Health Organization in 1961. Game-bird importers should be interested in the fact that one of the migratory birds carrying ticks that transmit serious human diseases was the coturnix quail.

This was the European variety of the bird, *Coturnix coturnix*, which has already been unsuccessfully introduced into the United States. It is also the one most likely to be given another trial when and if the coturnix quail comes up for its re-entrance examinations. The fact that it is now known to be a host of ticks capable of carrying such diseases as typhus and relapsing fever would seem a biological factor worthy of investigation before the bird is brought into the United States. It will be recalled that the initial coturnix shipment reaching Missouri in 1955 was of this same subspecies, live-trapped in Pakistan. Nor can we afford to comfort ourselves with the belief that the required three-week quarantine for incoming animals at the Department of Agriculture's Bureau of Animal Quarantine Station in New Jersey will always protect us against such sources of disease. Dr. Hoogstraal's research indicates that the birds might appear healthy throughout their quarantine period and still carry the ticks in immature form. He has pointed out that some species of ticks require from "several weeks to several months" to go through the immature stages, during which they are attached to the birds.

Especially disturbing is the fact that this coturnix-tick relationship was not known to those bringing the birds into this country in the 1950s. Dr. Hoogstraal started his bird research in 1956—a year after the coturnix from Pakistan were imported. It would be naïve to assume that we now know all there is to know about other disease-wildlife relationships.

A wildlife population not previously exposed to a disease may be much more subject to it than is the related species in the region where the disease originated. South American cottontails carried a strong resistance to myxomatosis which brought sudden death to rabbit populations elsewhere in the world. The chestnut blight, against which our native North American chestnut trees have proved so defenseless, is believed to have come in with an imported Oriental chestnut more resistant to the disease.

Parrots and parakeets, of which there are some 15,000,000 in the United States, are relatively resistant to parrot fever. But they have on occasion carried the hidden disease from their jungle homes and spread it among less-resistant people and wildlife. During the winter of 1929 and 1930 a new and serious outbreak of parrot fever, or ornithosis, occurred almost simultaneously in North America, North Africa, and Europe. In the United States there were 170 cases, thirty-three of them fatal. The total in the three areas was 750 cases, with 143 people dead. As various governments clamped down on regulations governing importation, quarantine, and sale of parrots and parakeets, the disease dropped off drastically. Pigeons also are known to carry parrot fever to humans, and in recent years starlings have become prime suspects. On March 28, 1959, sixty-four Boy Scouts turned out to clean the accumulated brush, leaves, and trash from a section of the city park in Mexico, Missouri. They piled the debris up for burning. In the previous nine years this section of the park had grown into a tangled jungle providing roosting space for thousands of starlings. Their droppings were thick over the ground. Two weeks after the big clean-up project, four of the Boy Scouts were ill with fever, high temperature, and coughing. Alert doctors, suspecting histoplasmosis, conducted skin tests and verified this diagnosis.

It is well authenticated that soils contaminated with pigeon and chicken droppings can be a source of infection of the organism causing this disease. Now it was suspected that starlings, too, could carry the organism in their droppings. All of the Boy Scouts were summoned to the hospital and given skin tests. All but two were positive.

With all these practical matters considered, there remains the question of whether or not transitory man, with his imperfect knowledge, has a right to mix up the animals of the earth as fits his whim and leave the results for succeeding generations. Or is this, like water pollution and strip mining, misuse of a natural resource that flaunts the long-range welfare of the human race?

What is the difference between bringing in a foreign species to run wild in the woods and fields and in bringing beef cattle to the Great Plains? There may be a bigger difference than some are willing to admit. Few of us would give up beef steaks, breakfast bacon, and fried chicken simply because they happen to be from introduced species. The Hereford steer, Suffolk sheep, Leghorn hen, and the human being who watches over them, are just as much exotics in this land as are the starling and the carp. The domestic animals, however, do live under severe controls many generations removed from their wild ancestry. Domesticated animals have an economic value to man which prompts him to fence them closely, guard them carefully, and count the new arrivals eagerly.

One biologist who leaves no doubt about his antipathy toward the introduction of foreign wildlife is Wisconsin's renowned ecologist and grouse authority, Dr. F. N. Hamerstrom, Jr. When it comes to the argument about domestic animals, Dr. Hamerstrom admits, "I can mostly rationalize that by saying it's all right to introduce domesticated plants and animals which are kept under cultivation and which cannot exist in the wild state—but there have been some nasty surprises there.

"The other extreme—and there are plenty of people who believe in it—is to mix everything up indiscriminately everywhere, so that every continent can have the advantage of whatever is good in another place; if the chamois is a fine thing in Europe, why shouldn't we have it, too? This," says Dr. Hamerstrom, "I find an appalling point of view. Even granting that undesirables could be kept out, or eliminated if they got in (neither is true), it still would leave us with an impoverished rather than an enriched existence. We cannot duplicate an ecological community simply by adding and subtracting species. And it should be quite plain that the more different communities we have, the richer we are; the more we downgrade variety into sameness, the poorer we become."

There might be areas of desert in the West, he concedes, where there are no native game birds or few birds of any kind and where an exotic bird could seemingly be added without harm. "In such a case it perhaps appears silly to be a purist," he says, "and yet I'm not so sure that it is silly. There have been wholly unexpected changes in behavior and in habitat tolerances in the past, plenty of them, and no man can be sure what will happen on the next try. For this reason if for no other I think it is proper to oppose introductions."

It is his opinion that "if we knew enough" about such questions as the imported animal's behavior in its new environment, its effect on plants, animals, and people, its side effects such as parasites and diseases, as well as the fact that it might serve some purpose, then in a cautious way it might be worth a try. "The hard fact remains, however," says Dr. Hamerstrom, "that we *don't* know enough and aren't apt to for a long, long time to come. It would be nice to have something more to shoot at," says Dr. Hamerstrom, an avid hunter as well as an ecologist, "but the risks are far too great."

It may be that what Dr. Tracy I. Storer, professor of zoology, University of California, said on the subject in 1931 is just as applicable today. ". . . it is my firm conviction," said Dr. Storer, "based upon two decades of study and observation of game problems in California, that our results to date in the attempted introduction and the acclimatization of game birds have not been worth the cost. The same amount of money, aggregating many thousands of dollars, devoted to *study and encouragement*, possibly even to propagation, of native species would have been productive of far greater results. . . ."

If we stand back from the subject of exotic animals far enough to see the over-all picture, and its historic ramifications, the record looks pathetic. Authoritative ecologists insist that we lack the answers, and we take grave risks when we propose to learn them by trial and error. There are vast gaps in our understanding of the biological communities. In an activity that could affect man and wildlife so profoundly for so long, we should hesitate to run the risk of new introductions where we cannot predict the outcome. And we cannot predict the outcome.

Dr. Herbert W. Levi of Harvard University's Museum of Comparative Zoology is one who is convinced that we are not even close to a time when our knowledge will make it safe to work with exotic animals. "No one," he states flatly, "can introduce exotic animals and forecast their biological effect. These introductions can never be on a scientific plane."

In spite of such opinions and the evidence supporting them, we have not yet enacted regulations adequate to insure us against the mistakes of the animal movers. Late in 1962, when the British motor ship *Athel Prince* came up the St. Lawrence Seaway and put in at the port of Duluth, one of the sailors aboard had a pet mongoose. He offered the smuggled mongoose to the Duluth Zoo, and the zoo director accepted it. His zoo thus became one of the few in the United States with the dubious honor of possessing a live mongoose.

Shortly, customs officials heard about the contraband animal. They called the Regional Office of the Bureau of Sport Fisheries and Wildlife in Minneapolis for instructions. Horrified wildlife specialists immediately dispatched an order to the Duluth Zoo. The Lacey Act of 1900 stipulated that the predatory mongoose must be either destroyed or deported. The zoo director, instead of complying, permitted local newspapers to learn of the plight of his condemned animal. Meanwhile, city attorneys began checking the federal laws for a loophole.

Duluth newspapers gave the mongoose a name; they called him "Mr. Magoo." Public indignation flared. Here was a little furred creature—all alone in the world, devoid of hope, victim of a heartless government. Poor Mr. Magoo!

While wildlife officials in Minneapolis and Washington fretted, the mongoose's defense attorneys in Duluth informed the mayor that the law, as they understood it, permitted the Secretary of the Interior, providing certain conditions of captivity were met, to issue a special permit to keep the animal for zoological display. This, although true, ignored the fact that the animal had entered illegally. On November 16, 1962, the mayor of Duluth rushed a wire to Washington requesting the Secretary to make an "administrative exception." The mayor pointed out that ". . . public reaction to the execution order here is positively fantastic." Other politicians were by now in contact with the Secretary to plead for the mongoose on behalf of their animal-loving constituents.

The Secretary stalled, but pressure grew and on December 8 he sent the mayor of Duluth a letter saying the city could keep its cherished exotic predator temporarily until March 1, 1963. The permit was later extended indefinitely. What was not widely known at the time was that the sailor who originally donated the animal had brought in not one, but two mongooses. Fortunately, one of the animals had died before the ship docked. The specter of a pair of fertile mongooses loose on the North American mainland is enough to unnerve most wildlife biologists.

One lesson growing from this affair is that public officials should not have to weave their way through a maze of legal details or yield to pressures and permit unwanted animals asylum in the United States. The laws should be clearly prohibitive concerning such creatures as the mongoose, and not permissive. The decision in such a case should not be a matter left to the discretion of the officeholder at any given moment in history.

This affair of Mr. Magoo also emphasizes the general weakness of regulations over the importation of wildlife into the United States. Such laws as do exist leave the final decisions in the hands of individual officeholders—usually those in the state game and fish departments. This, unfortunately, is the way most state game and fish administrators want it to remain. They look upon wildlife transplanting as a matter of states' rights.

By this time in our history we should have worked out better laws to protect wildlife and humans from the gambling instincts of the animal movers. We should look upon wildlife management as more than an exercise in rearrangement, because history tells us, and science assures us, that transplanting a wild creature to a new environment is a delicate and hazardous business. Too often, however, we are still inclined to see the world of nature as modeling clay and man as the sculptor. This is not to say there never should be a species moved to a new area. But just as the acclimatizers of the 1800s could ship sparrows around the world, so can citizens and government agencies today turn out foreign wild creatures in far more places than they should. One of the justifications advanced for establishing the federal government's exotic wildlife program was that it might as well be organized because, "Introductions are coming in whether we like it or not."

The sincerity and good intentions of the animal transplanters are seldom questioned. But sincerity is not enough. And good intentions brought the United States house sparrows, starlings, and carp, took North American gray squirrels and muskrats to Europe, and European rabbits to Australia and New Zealand.

When a state does begin thinking about a new exotic animal, the accompanying urge to seek publicity in advance of the results seems irresistible. A coturnix quail, striped bass, or giant kudu project is good for three to fifteen years of publicity. News media are fed a regular diet of releases keeping the hopeful public constantly appraised of the state's progress in creating new hunting and fishing oportunities with the latest exotic cure-all.

In May 1965 the Michigan Conservation Department issued a news release announcing in advance the approaching initial stocking of kokanee salmon into Michigan waters. The fish were not released quietly nor in the scientific atmosphere that might befit an untested research project. Among the dignitaries present was Governor George Romney to dump the first pailful of kokanee salmon into Torch Lake while wishing them well in a most public fashion. Such affairs condition outdoorsmen to continue looking with favor upon exotic wild creatures. We are steadily anesthetized against painful memories of exotic wildlife disasters and failures. Too often we ask only whether or not the foreign species can live in this country, and too seldom question whether or not native species can live with them.

Partly because they cling to their control over exotics, the state administrators sometimes find themselves in difficult situations that endanger neighboring states as well. During the San Juan rabbit craze of the 1950s, Ohio's chief of game management, Dr. E. D. Martin, was quoted in the public press as saying, "We have not prohibited the importation of this rabbit and we don't plan to do so right away. Anybody can get permission to bring them in.

"We know what damage they have done in other areas so we have been trying to discourage their importation here. Still, until we have bonafide evidence as to their danger to the economy or their lack of danger, we're not going to stick our necks out one way or the other."

If the state game and fish commission requires permits for wildlife introductions, these are frequently arranged with great ease. Some states lack any authority to control the whims of citizens who decide to release exotic wildlife. As late as August 1964, a representative of the Utah Department of Game and Fish was able to say, "At present, the Utah Department of Game and Fish does not have the legislative authority to exclude any species from introduction by private citizens." Missouri's regulations are typical. That state's wildlife code says, "No wildlife of any kind may be liberated unless specific permission has been granted on written application to the conservation agent in the district where the release is to be made." In Michigan, which has a similar rule, the person importing most unauthorized wildlife risks only having the animals confiscated. But he can be fined $500 and spend two years in jail for using a slug in a public telephone.

California's record on control of imported exotics is better than that of many states. On August 15, 1895, five years before the Lacey Act, California's State Board of Horticulture adopted a regulation saying, in part, ". . . animals known as flying fox (the fruit bat), Australian or English wild rabbit, or other animals or birds detrimental to fruit or fruit trees, plants, etc., are prohibited from being brought or landed in this state, and, if brought, they shall be destroyed."

Following the passage of this law, port authorities in California detected, seized, and destroyed several flying foxes. It also led to the seizure and destruction of almost every mongoose known to have arrived in California, and it is altogether possible that, except for this single law, and the efficiency of port authorities at San Francisco, the mongoose might be running wild over a sizable part of this country today.

The California Department of Fish and Game publishes a lengthy list of species which may not be imported to the state except under special conditions. Citizens, however, may readily get permission to turn out coturnix quail, Barbary partridge, chukar partridge, and red-legged partridges.

The first effort of the United States government to control release of foreign wildlife came with passage of the Lacey Act on May 25, 1900. Section 2 of that act stated that "it shall be unlawful for any person or persons to import into the United States any foreign wild animal or bird except under special permit from the United States Department of Agriculture." The act specifically prohibited the importation of the mongoose, starling, English sparrow, fruit bat, and other species the Secretary of Agriculture might consider harmful to agriculture or horticulture. Later changes gave authority for administration of the law to the Secretary of the Interior. Amendments over the years introduced exceptions which have had the effect of weakening, not strengthening, the act. The Secretary of the Interior has authority under certain circumstances, to approve importation even of those animals specifically barred by the original legislation. With our inadequate hodgepodge of permissive rules, federal and state, the animal transplanters still have little to slow them down in their everlasting chess game.

Meanwhile, with each passing generation we add to the evidence that such importations should not be left to the desires of any individual mainland state. Nor should such decisions be left to a single nation alone in those cases where the country shares a land mass with other countries.

Wild populations, or diseases that might come with them, cannot be expected to stop at state borders. Even if one state were to prohibit release of European hedgehogs, there would be little to keep an adjoining state from turning the hedgehogs out five feet from the state line. The Great Lakes and the St. Lawrence River draining them touch on eight states and three Canadian provinces, with dozens of streams reaching like tentacles back into the interior watershed. Yet there is no law, treaty, or agreement to prevent one state from introducing a new fish—including one as potentially damaging as the carp—into its portion of the interconnected waterway.

The real need is for an international board of highly qualified scientists to weigh and rule on applications for the release of exotics into new territories. Such an international approach was recommended in 1956 by Dr. Antoon De Vos, then of Ontario Agricultural College, Dr. Richard G. Van Gelder of The American Museum of Natural History, and naturalist Dr. Richard H. Manville, writing in *Zoologica*. Dr.

C. Richard Robins of the Institute of Marine Science favors establishing an international advisory board with representatives of all the professional societies concerned with various classifications of wildlife. Such a group, composed of the best-qualified ecologists, parasitologists, and other specialists, could have subcommittees charged with the responsibility of approving or rejecting suggestions for importation of mammals, birds, fish, reptiles, amphibians, and invertebrates.

Establishing such a board and granting it authority would help protect states and nations from the mistakes of their neighbors. It would strengthen the controls and slow down the age-old pastime of wildlife reshuffling. It could bring added protection to future generations, both of human and wild populations.

Otherwise we can expect to watch what remains of the wild natural communities be polluted by the capercaillie from Europe, the oryx from Africa, or the marsupials from Australia all mingled and mixed by the human being from God knows where.

As things now stand, we look away from our magnificent heritage of native wildlife and its habitat to cast covetous glances at strange creatures in far corners of the world. Then, ignoring the lessons of the past, we start another round of wildlife roulette.

Bibliography and Further Reading

GENERAL

ALLEN, D. L. 1954. Our wildlife legacy. New York: Funk & Wagnalls Co.

ANDERSON, R. M. 1933. Effect of the introduction of exotic animal forms. Proc. Fifth Pacific Sci. Cong., 1:769–778.

ANDREWS, J. D. 1953. The danger of wildlife introductions. Garden Gossip, March.

ANON. 1944. Hits, misses, and home runs. Penna. Game News, 15 (4):4–5, 28, 30.

BIGALKE, R. 1937. The naturalization of animals, with special reference to South Africa. S. Afr. Jour. Sci., 33:45–63.

1937. The adulteration of the fauna and flora of our national parks. S. Afr. Jour. Sci., 43:221–225.

BLOUCH, R. I. 1954. Introductions all around. Mich. Conservation. 23 (3):6–9.

BUMP, G. 1940. The introduction and transplantation of game birds and mammals into the state of New York. Fifth North American Wildlife Conference, 5:409–420.

CAHALANE, V. H. 1955. Some effects of exotics on nature. Proc. International Technical Conference on Nature Protection, UNESCO, 396–405.

CARL, G. and GUIGUET, C. J. 1958. Alien Animals in British Columbia, B. C. Prov. Museum, Handbook No. 14. 94 pp.

CLARK, A. H. 1949. The invasion of New Zealand by people, plants, and animals. Rutgers University Press.

COTTAM, C. 1950. The effect of uncontrolled introductions of plants and animals. Proc. and Papers International Technical Conference on Protection of Nature, UNESCO:408–413.

DAY, A. M. 1948. Introduction of exotic species. U. S. Department of the Interior, Fish and Wildlife Serv. 13 pp.

DUVIGNEAUD, P. 1949. The introduction of exotic species. International Technical Conference on Protection of Nature. UNESCO.

HICKS, L. E. 1940. The role of exotics in the Ohio Valley. Trans. Fifth North American Wildlife Conference, 420–424.

LEVI, H. W. 1952. Evaluation of wildlife importations. Scientific Monthly, 74:315–322.

LINDEMANN, W. 1956. Transplantation of game in Europe and Asia. Jour. Wildlife Mgt., 20:68–70.

MURIE, O. J. 1940. Wildlife in Alaska. Trans. Fifth North American Wildlife Conference. 432–436.

OSBORN, T. A. B. 1933. Effect of introductions of exotic plants and animals into Australia. Proc. Fifth Pacific Sci. Cong., 1:809–810.

PALMER, T. S. 1899. The danger of introducing noxious animals and birds. U. S. Dept. of Agriculture Yearbook for 1898: 87–110.

RUHL, H. D. 1940. Game introductions into Michigan. Trans. Fifth North American Wildlife Conference, 424–427.

STEEN, M. O. 1953. Report of the committee on exotic animals. Proc. 42nd Convention International Association Game, Fish and Conservation Commissioners.

STORER, T. I. 1931. Known and potential results of bird and animal introductions with special reference to California. Calif. Dept. Agriculture Monthly Bulletin, 20:267–273.

——— 1933. Economic effects of introducing alien animals into California. Proc. Fifth Pacific Sci. Congress, 1:779–784.

SWANSON, G. A. 1949. The need for research in the introduction of exotic animals. International Technical Conference on Protection of Nature. UNESCO.

THOMSON, G. M. 1922. The naturalization of animals and plants in New Zealand. Cambridge Univ. Press, 607 pp.

——— 1923. Naturalized animals and plants. New Zealand Jour. of Science and Technology, 6:223–231.

WESTERKOV, K. 1952. Acclimatization of new game species. New Zealand Dept. Internal Affairs. Wildlife Publication. 17:1–8.

MAMMALS

ANON. 1952. Wild burros in California. Outdoor California, 13 (25):4–5.

———1953. California's wild burros given legal protection. Outdoor California, 14 (20):2.

———1953. Iceland's mink are a menace to wildlife. Modern Game Breeding and Hunting Club News. 23 (8):13.

——1954. A new threat: European rabbits in the U. S. Nature Conserv. News, 4 (5):1.

——1955. Set special seasons on Barbary sheep. New Mexico Magazine, 33 (11):31–33.

——1961. Status of feral burros in Calif. Calif. Dept. of Fish & Game. Aug.

——1963. Mongoose at Duluth Zoo gets full federal pardon, news release, U. S. Dept. of the Interior, Apr. 20.

AHRENS, T. G. 1921. Muskrats in central Europe. Jour. Mammalogy, 2:236–237.

ALLIN, A. E. 1950. European hare introduced into the district of Thunder Bay, Ontario. Canadian Field Naturalist, 64:122–124.

ASHBROOK, F. G. 1953. Muskrat-nutria. Louisiana Conservationist, 5 (6): 16–17.

BAILEY, A. M. and HENDEE, R. W. 1926. Notes on the mammals of northwestern Alaska. Jour. Mammalogy, 7:9–28.

BAILEY, H. H. 1924. The armadillo in Florida and how it reached there. Jour. Mammalogy, 5:264–265.

BALDWIN, P. H. et al. 1952. Life history and economic status of the mongoose in Hawaii. Jour. Mammalogy, 33:335–356.

BARNES, W. B. 1955. Status of the San Juan rabbit in the Midwest. Trans. Seventeenth Midwest Wildlife Conference.

BEDNARIK, K. 1955. The San Juan rabbit: Furred Menace? Ohio Conservation Bulletin, Dec.:8–9.

BLOEKER, J. C. VON. 1928. Records of opossums from San Diego County. Jour. Mammalogy, 9:62.

BOURDELLE, E. 1939. American mammals introduced into France in the contemporary period, especially Myocastor and Ondatra. Jour. Mammalogy, 20:287–291.

BROCKIE, R. E. Observation on the food of the hedgehog in New Zealand. N. Z. Jour. Sci. 2:121–36.

BRYAN, L. W. 1937. Wild pigs in Hawaii. Paradise of the Pacific, 49 (12):31–32.

BRYANT, H. C. 1927. Opossum depredations increasing. California Fish & Game, 13:127.

    1927. The opossum reaches San Diego County. California Fish & Game, 13:146.

BUCHANAN, G. D. 1955. Nine-banded armadillo-invader from the south. Animal Kingdom, 58 (3):82–88.

BULL, P. C. 1953. Parasites of the wild rabbit Oryctolagus cuniculus in New Zealand, New Zealand Jour. Science & Technology, Sec. B, 34:341–372.

    1964. Ecology of Helminth Parasites of the wild rabbit Oryctola-

gus cuniculus in New Zealand, N. Z. Dept. Scientific and Industrial Research Bull. 158.

COUCH, L. K. 1929. Introduced European rabbits in the San Juan Islands, Washington. Jour. Mammalogy, 10:334–336.

DAVIS, G. S. 1953. Respite for the burro. Nature Magazine, 46 (7): 370–374.

DE VOS, A., MANVILLE, R. H., and VAN GELDER, R. G. 1956. Introduced mammals and their influence on native biota. Zoologica. 41 (4):163–194.

DICE, L. R. 1927. The transfer of game and fur-bearing mammals from state to state, with special reference to the cotton-tail rabbit. Jour. Mammalogy, 8:90–96.

———. 1952. Natural Communities. University of Michigan Press.

DICKEY, D. R. 1923. An extension of the range of the muskrat in California. Jour. Mammalogy, 4:55–56.

DIXON, J. S. 1929. Artificial distribution of fur-bearing mammals. Jour. Mammalogy, 10:358–359.

DOZIER, H. L. 1951. The present status and future of nutria in the Southeastern States. Fifth annual meeting, Southeastern Assn. Game & Fish Commissioners.

ESPEUT, W. B. 1882. On the acclimatization of the Indian mongoose in Jamaica. Proc. Zool. Society, 712–714.

EYERDAM, W. J. 1932. A shipment of muskrats to Kamchatka, Jour. Mammalogy, 13:281–282.

FITCH, H. S., GOODRUM, P. and NEWMAN, C. 1952. The armadillo in the Southeastern United States. Jour. Mammalogy, 33:21–37.

FLEMING, W. L. 1909. Jefferson Davis's camel experiment. Pop. Sci. Feb.

FRASER, F. 1953. Wildlife management in the Yukon Territory. Forestry Chron., 29 (2):150–157.

FULWIDER, D. S. 1965. Bakersfield's boom in burros. Our Public Lands —BLM—U. S. Dept. of the Interior. 14 (4):14–15.

GLASS, B. P. and HANSON, W. R. 1952. A feral coatimundi in northwestern Oklahoma. Jour. Mammalogy, 33:108–109.

HANSON, H. C. 1952. Importance and development of the reindeer industry in Alaska. Jour. Range Management, 5 (4):243–251.

HARRIS, VAN T. 1956. Transactions. Twenty-first North American Wildlife Conference, 474–486.

HAWDEN, S. J. and PALMER, L. J. 1922. Reindeer in Alaska. U. S. Dept. of Agriculture Bulletin, 1089:74.

HOCK, R. J. 1952. The opossum in Arizona. Jour. Mammalogy, 33: 464–470.

HOWARD, W. E. 1953. Nutria *Myocastor coypus* in California, Jour. Mammalogy, 34 (4):512–513.

1959. The rabbit problem in New Zealand. Dept. of Scientific and Industrial Research Information Series No. 16. 47 pp.

JACKSON, HARTLEY H. J. 1961. Mammals of Wisconsin. Univ. of Wisc. Press.

JELLISON, W. L. 1945. Spotted skunk and feral nutria in Montana. Jour. Mammalogy, 26:432.

JEWETT, S. G. and DOBYNS, H. W. 1929. The Virginia opossum in Oregon. Jour. Mammalogy, 10:351.

JONES, P. 1959. The European wild boar in North Carolina. N. C. Wildlife Resources Comm. 30 pp.

KLEIN, D. R. 1959. Saint Matthew Island reindeer-range study. U. S. Dept. of the Interior, Fish and Wildlife Service. Special Scientific Report—Wildlife No. 43. 48 pp.

KOEHLER, J. W. 1960. The California undomesticated burro. The Bulletin, Calif. Dept. of Agriculture XLIX: No. 1.

LANTIS, M. 1950. The reindeer industry in Alaska. Arctic, 3 (1): 27–44.

LARRISON, E. J. 1943. Feral coypus in the Pacific Northwest. Murrelet, 24:3–9.

LATHAM, R. M. 1954. The San Juan rabbit. Pa. Game News. Sept.

LEE, L. New Mexico's exotic game program. N. M. Dept. of Game & Fish. Not dated.

LEHMANN, V. W. 1948. Restocking on King Ranch. Transactions Thirteenth North American Wildlife Conference, 236–242.

LEWIS, C. B. 1953. Rats and the mongoose in Jamaica. Oryx, 2 (3): 170–172.

LITTLE, E. V. 1916. The opossum in Los Angeles County. California Fish & Game, 2:46–47.

LOMEN, C. J. 1919. The camel of the frozen desert (reindeer). National Geographic Magazine 36 (6):538–556.

LYON, M. W. JR. 1923. A stray coati in Indiana. Jour. Mammalogy, 4:184–185.

MIDDLETON, A. D. 1930. The ecology of the American gray squirrel *Sciurus carolinensis* Gmelin in the British Isles. Proc. Zool. Society, London, 809–849.

MOHR, E. 1933. The muskrat, *Ondatra zibethica* (Linnaeus), in Europe. Jour. Mammalogy, 14:58–63.

MURIE, O. J. 1940. Wildlife introductions in Alaska. Trans. Fifth North American Wildlife Conference, 532–536.

MYERS, J. G. 1931. The present position of the mongoose in the West Indies. Tropical Agriculture, 8 (4):94–95.

NEILL, W. T. 1952. The spread of the armadillo in Florida. Ecology, 33:282–284.

O'CONNOR, J. 1953. The bearded Texan. Outdoor Life. 112 (2): 44–45, 91–92 (Barbary Sheep).

OGREN, H. A. 1962. Barbary sheep in New Mexico. N. M. Dept. of Game & Fish, Bulletin No. 11. 32 pp.

PACKARD, R. L. 1955. Release, dispersal and reproduction of fallow deer in Nebraska. Jour. Mammalogy, 36:471–473.

PALMER, L. J. and ROUSE, C. H. 1945. Study of the Alaska tundra with reference to its reactions to reindeer and other grazing. Res. Report 10. U. S. Dept. of the Interior. 48 pp.

PETRIDES, G. A. 1950. The nutria comes to Texas. Texas Game & Fish, May:4–5.

PIMENTEL, D. 1955. Biology of the Indian mongoose in Puerto Rico. Jour. Mammalogy, 36:62–68.

1955. The control of the mongoose in Puerto Rico. American Jour. of Tropical Medicine & Hygiene. 4 (1):147–151.

PULLAR, E. M. 1953. The wild (feral) pigs of Australia; their origin, distribution and economic importance. Mem. Nat. Mus. Melbourne, 18:7–23.

RUTHERFORD, J. G., MCLEAN, J. S. and HARKIN, J. B. 1922. Reindeer and musk-ox. Ottawa. Dept. of Interior. 1–99. pp.

SALVESEN, S. 1928. The beaver in Norway. Jour. Mammalogy, 9: 99–104.

SCHEFFER, V. B. 1941. Management studies on transplanted beavers in the Pacific Northwest. Trans. Sixth North American Wildlife Conference, 320–326.

1943. The opossum settles in Washington, State Murrelet, 24: 27–28.

1947. Raccoons transplanted in Alaska. Jour. Wildlife Management, 11 (4):350–351.

1951. The rise and fall of a reindeer herd. Scientific Monthly, 74:356–362.

SEAMEN, G. A. 1952. The mongoose and Caribbean wildlife. Seventeenth North American Wildlife Conference, 188–197.

SHAW, A. C. 1940. The European wild hog in America. Trans. Fifth North American Wildlife Conference. 436–441.

SHERMAN, H. D. 1954. Raccoons of the Bahama Islands. Jour. Mammalogy, 35:126.

SHORTEN, M. 1946. A survey of the distribution of the American gray squirrel (*Sciurus carolinensis*) and the British red squirrel

(*Sciurus vulgaris leucourus*) in England and Wales in 1944–5. Jour. Animal Ecology, 15:82–92.

1953. Notes on the distribution of the gray squirrel (*Sciurus carolinensis*) and the red squirrel (*Sciurus vulgaris leucourus*) in England and Wales. Jour. Animal Ecology, 22:134–140.

1964. Introduced menace (gray squirrel in Great Britain). Nat. History Magazine. 10:43–48.

STEGEMAN, L. C. 1938. The European wild boar in the Cherokee National Forest, Tennessee. Jour. Mammalogy, 19:279–290.

STORER, T. I. 1937. The muskrat as native and alien. Jour. Mammalogy. 18:443–460.

SUMNER, LOWELL. 1959. Transactions of Third Annual Meeting, Desert Bighorn Council, Death Valley, California, 4.

SWANK, W. G. and PETRIDES, G. A. 1954. Establishment and food habits of the nutria in Texas. Ecology, 35:172–175.

THOMPSON, H. V. 1955. The wild European rabbit and possible dangers of its introduction into the U.S.A. Jour. Wildlife Management, 19:8–13.

TIERKEL, E. S. et al. 1952. Mongoose rabies in Puerto Rico. Public Health Reports, 67 (3):274–278.

TROUGHTON, E. LEG. 1938. Australian mammals: their past and future. Jour. Mammalogy, 19:401–411.

TUBBS, C. L. 1916. The opossum in Amador County. California Fish & Game, 2:111.

TURCEK, F. J. 1951. Effect of introductions on two game populations in Czechoslovakia. Jour. Wildlife Management. 15 (1):113–114.

WARWICK, T. 1934. The distribution of the muskrat (*Fiber zibethicus*) in the British Isles. Jour. Animal Ecology, 3:250–267.

WATSON, J. S. 1961. Feral rabbit populations on Pacific Islands. Pacific Science Vol. XV, No. 4. Oct.

WILDHAGEN, A. 1956. Present distribution of North American mink in Norway. Jour. Mammalogy, 37:116–118.

WODZICKI, K. A. 1950. Introduced mammals of New Zealand. Dept. Scientific and Industrial Research. Bulletin No. 98:250 pp.

BIRDS

ABARBANEL, A. 1959. Pigeons aren't pets—they're pests. Today's Health, July: 74–75.

ALDRICH, J. W. et al. 1961. Bird hazard to aircraft, U. S. Fish and Wildlife Service. Wlf. Leaflet 429.

ALLEN, D. L. 1956. Pheasants in North America, The Stackpole Co. 490 pp.

ANON. 1873. Introduction of European birds in the United States for economic purposes. Zoologist 2nd Ser., 8:3696.

——1874. The introduction of singing birds into the country. (U.S.) Forest & Stream, 2:264.

——1881. Zoological Miscellany, Jour. Cincinnati Society of Natural History. IV.

——1949. Conduct Wisconsin tests with European grouse. Wisconsin Con. Bulletin. Oct:35.

——1954. Brown francolins may give international flavor to hunting. Arizona Game & Fish Dept. Wildlife News, 1 (1):6.

——1956. The Coturnix quail. Leaflet No. 1–56. Ohio Division of Wildlife.

——1958. Red-legged partridges of Spain. Special Sci. Report—Wlf. No. 39. U. S. Fish and Wildlife Service.

——1961. Birds and the spread of disease. WHO Chronicle, Vol. 15, No. 7.

——1961. Migratory birds carry diseases overseas. Sci. News Letter, 80:321. Nov. 11.

——1962. Bird-borne diseases in man. What's new. Abbott Laboratories. Summer.

——1962. The foreign game introduction program. Conservation Backgrounds, U. S. Fish and Wildlife Service, Mar. 19.

——1963. Battle against Cryptococcosis. M.D. Nov.

——1963. Kill those pigeons, Time. Oct. 18.

——1963. Status of the foreign game introduction program. Trans. Twenty-eighth North American Wildlife and Natural Resources Conference. 240–247.

BOHL, W. H. 1957. Chukars in New Mexico. Bulletin No. 6, N. M. Dept. of Game and Fish. 68 pp.

BRAVERMAN, M. M. et al. 1962. The contribution to air pollution by pigeons. Jour. of the Air Pollution Assn. 12 (12) Dec.

BRYAN, W. A. 1912. The introduction and acclimatization of the yellow canary on Midway Island. The Auk, 29:339–342.

BUMP, G. 1940. The introduction and transplantation of game birds and mammals into the State of New York. Trans. North American Wildlife Conference, 5:409–420.

1951. Game introductions—when, where, and how. Trans. Sixteenth North American Wildlife Conference, 316–325.

1952. How shall foreign species be introduced? Atlantic Naturalist. 7 (3):112–117.

1964. (With Bohl, W. H.) Summary of foreign game bird propagation and liberations 1960 to 1963. Special Scientific Report—Wildlife No. 80. Bureau of Sport Fisheries and Wildlife, 48 pp.

CHRISTENSEN, G. C. 1954. The Chukar partridge in Nevada. Nev. Fish and Game Commission. Biol. Bulletin No. 1, 77 pp.

1963. Sand grouse released in Nevada found in Mexico. The Condor. 65 (1) 67–68.

1964. (With Bohl, W. H.) A study and review of the common Indian sand grouse. Special scientific report—Wildlife No. 84. Bureau of Sport Fisheries and Wildlife.

EHRHORN, E. M. 1925. Bird introductions into Hawaii. Hawaii Board of Agriculture and Forestry, Report for 1924: 42–43.

FISHER, H. I. 1948. The question of avian introductions in Hawaii. Pacific Science, 2:59–64.

GERSTELL, R. 1940. The Hungarian and chukar partridges in Pa. Trans. Fifth. North American Wildlife Conference.

HALAZON, G. 1949. A study in the introduction, release and survival of capercaillie and black grouse. Wis. Wildlife Research Quarterly Progress Report, 8 (3):92–97.

1950. Capercaillie and black grouse research. Wis. Wildlife Research Quarterly Progress Report, 8 (4):92–97.

HAMERSTROM, F. and HAMERSTROM F. 1963. The symposium in review. Jour. Wildlife Management. 27 (4):868–887.

HOLMGREN, V. C. 1964. Chinese pheasants, Oregon Pioneers. Oregon Historical Quarterly, LXV (3):229–262.

HOOGSTRAAL, H. et al. 1961. Ticks (lxodoides) on birds migrating from Africa to Europe and Asia. Bulletin WHO 24:197.

KEEFE, J. 1955. Coturnix quail—a new Missouri game bird? Missouri Cons., 16 (7):12–13.

KING, R. T. 1942. Is it a wise policy to introduce exotic game birds? Audubon Magazine, 44:136–145, 230–236, 306–310.

KIRKPATRICK, R. D. 1959. Coturnix investigation final report P-R Proj. Indiana Dept. of Conservation.

MCATEE, W. L. 1925. Introduction upon introduction. The Auk., 42: 160.

1929. Game birds suitable for naturalizing in the United States. Dept. of Agriculture Circular, 96:1–23.

MERRIAM, C. H. 1889. The English sparrow in North America. U. S. Dept. of Agriculture Bulletin 1.

MILLER, L. 1930. The Asiatic mynah in Los Angeles, Calif. Condor, 32:302.

MYRES, M. T. 1958. The European starling in British Columbia, B. C. Provincial Museum, Occasional papers, No. 11.

NORTHWOOD, J. D'A. 1952. The myna in Hawaii, asset or liability. Audubon Magazine, 55:22–27.

NOSEK, J. et al. 1962. The role of birds in a natural focus of tick-borne encephalitis. Jour. of Hygiene, Epidemiology, Microbiology and Immunology, VI. 478.

PALMER, T. S. and OLDYS, H. 1904. Importation of game birds and eggs for propagation. U. S. Dept. of Agriculture Farmers' Bulletin No. 198. 1–27.

PHILLIPS, J. C. 1928. Wild birds introduced or transplanted in North America. U. S. Dept. of Agriculture Technical Bulletin No. 61:1–63.

PIERCE, R. A. 1956. Some thoughts concerning the introduction of exotic game birds. Wilson Bulletin, 68 (1):81–82.

PORTER, R. D. 1955. The Hungarian partridge in Utah. Jour. Wildlife Mgt., 19:93–108.

SALTER, R. L. 1952. Chukar partridge introductions in Idaho. 1952 Proc. Western Association Fish and Game Commissioners.

SCHEFFER, T. H. 1955. Present status of the introduced English skylark on Vancouver Island and of the Chinese mynah on the Vancouver mainland. Murrelet, 36 (2):28–29.

SCHWARTZ, C. W. and SCHWARTZ, E. R. 1949. The game birds in Hawaii. Board of Agr. and Forestry, Hawaii. 168 pp.

SEAMAN, G. A. 1952. The mongoose and Caribbean wildlife. Seventeenth North American Wildlife Conference. 188–197.

STANFORD, J. A. 1957. A progress report of coturnix quail investigations in Missouri. Transactions of the twenty-second North American Wildlife Conference, 316–359.

STONER, D. 1923. The mynah—a study in adaptation. Auk., 40:328–330.

SUMMERS-SMITH, J. D. 1963. The house sparrow, Collins, London.

TAVERNER, P. A. 1927. Hungarian partridge vs. sharptailed grouse. Canad. Field Naturalist, 41:147–149.

WESTERKOV, K. 1949. Scandinavian grouse. A discussion of the suitability of the Northern Peninsula for them. Michigan Conservation, March–April:26–31.

1953. Introduction into New Zealand of the Australian blue wren in 1923. Notornis, 5 (3):106–107.

FISH

ALBRECHT, A. B. 1964. Some observations on factors associated with survival of striped bass eggs and larvae. Calif. Fish & Game. 50 (2):April. 100–113.

ANON. 1953. More wrongs will not make it right. Montana Wildlife. 3 (3):4–5.

FERGUSON, A. D. 1915. Extending the range of the golden trout. Trans. Pacific Fish. Soc., 1916:65–70.

KELLY, H. D. 1956. Preliminary studies on *Tilapia mossambica* Peters relative to experimental pond culture. Proc. Tenth Annual Conference SE Association Game & Fish Commissioners.

MYERS, G. 1925. Introduction of the European bitterling (*Rhodeus*) in New York and of the rudd (*Scardinius*) in New Jersey. Copeia, No. 140:20–21.

NEALE, G. 1922. Black bass shipment to Mexico. California Fish & Game, 8 (2):114–117.

RAWSON, D. S. 1946. The experimental introduction of smallmouth black bass into lakes of the Prince Albert National Park, Saskatchewan. Trans. American Fish. Soc. (1943), 73:19–31.

STEVENS, R. E. 1957. The striped bass of the Santee-Cooper reservoir. Proc. Eleventh Annual Conf. SE Association Fish & Game Commissioners. 253–264.

THOMPSON, F. A. 1940. Salmonoid fishes in the Argentine Andes. Trans. American Fish. Soc. 69 (1939):279–284.

INVERTEBRATES

ABBOT, R. T. 1949. March of giant African snail. Natural History Magazine. Feb:68.
1950. Snail invaders. Natural History Magazine, Feb: 80–85.

ALEXANDER, R. C. 1952. Introduced species of land snails in New Jersey. Nautilus, 65:132–135.

EMMETT, W. P. 1956. Liver flukes of cattle and sheep. Yearbook, U. S. Department of Agriculture. 148–153.

FERGUSON, F. F. et al. 1960. National abatement of Schistosomiasis Mansoni in St. Kitts, British West Indies. Public Health. April. 261–265.

HANNA, G. D. 1939. Exotic mollusca in Calif. Bulletin California Dept. of Agriculture. May. XXVIII:298–321.

INGRAM, W. M. 1952. Thousands of living European snails sold as fish bait in the State of Ohio. Nautilus 66:26–29.

LOOSANOFF, V. L. 1955. The European oyster in American waters. Science, 121:119–121.

MEAD, A. R. 1961. The giant African snail, Univ. of Chicago Press.

PANNING, A. 1939. The Chinese mitten crab. Ann. Report Smithsonian Institution, 1938:361–375.

RITCHIE, L. S. et al. 1962. Population dynamics of *Australorbis glabratus* in Puerto Rico. Bulletin WHO 27:171–181.

WILLIAMS, F. X. 1951. Life history studies of East African *Achatina* snails. Bulletin Mus. Comp. Zool., 105:293–317.

GEORGE LAYCOCK is a full-time free-lance writer on outdoor subjects and, since 1951, has had articles appearing in every major outdoor magazine in the United States. A lifetime resident of Ohio and a graduate of Ohio State University with a degree in wildlife management, he was formerly an associate editor for the *Farm Quarterly* and a member of the Ohio Wildlife Council.

In the course of his travels for ideas and research, travels which have often included his wife and three children, he has covered the Western Hemisphere north beyond the Arctic Circle and as far south as Chile and Argentina. He is a member of the Wilderness Society, the Wildlife Society, The National Parks Association, the Outdoor Writers of America, and the Society of Magazine Writers, and the author of four previous books, including *The Deer Hunter's Bible* and the very popular *The Sign of the Flying Goose: A Guide to the National Wildlife Refuges*, published by the Natural History Press in 1965.

Index